CAMBRIDGE SCHO[...]

Shakespeare

Shakespeare's Language

150 PHOTOCOPIABLE WORKSHEETS

Rex Gibson

CAMBRIDGE
UNIVERSITY PRESS

PUBLISHED BY THE PRESS SYNDICATE OF THE UNIVERSITY OF CAMBRIDGE
The Pitt Building, Trumpington Street, Cambridge, United Kingdom

CAMBRIDGE UNIVERSITY PRESS
The Edinburgh Building, Cambridge CB2 2RU, UK
40 West 20th Street, New York, NY 10011–4211, USA
477 Williamstown Road, Port Melbourne, VIC 3207, Australia
Ruiz de Alarcón 13, 28014 Madrid, Spain
Dock House, The Waterfront, Cape Town 8001, South Africa

http://www.cambridge.org

First published 1997
Fifth printing 2003

Printed in the United Kingdom at the University Press, Cambridge

A catalogue record for this book is available from the British Library.

ISBN 0 521 57811 6

Prepared for publication by Paren & Stacey Editorial Consultants
Designed by Richard Morris, Stonesfield Design
Art editing and picture research by Jane Taylor

Illustrations by Gerry Grace (pages 3, 23, 24, 30, 59, 73, 78, 85, 103, 117); Adam Stower (pages 15, 21, 26, 39, 42, 52, 53, 56, 66, 80, 88, 96, 107, 118, 127, 137); Sarah Young (2, 4, 16, 18, 50, 54, 62, 69, 79, 82, 89, 92, 98, 99, 102, 109, 110, 112, 125, 132, 133, 141)

Thanks are due to the following for permission to reproduce photographs: The Globe Theatre, detail from an engraving, 1616 by Cornelius de Visscher (1619/29–62) British Library, London/Bridgeman Art Library, London, page 5; Proportions of the human figure, c.1482 (Vitruvian Man) by Leonardo da Vinci (1452–1519) Galleria dell' Accademia, Venice/Bridgeman Art Library, London, page 44; Donald Cooper/Photostage, RSC 1982, page 45; ET Archive, pages 29 (Tate Gallery) and 81; Mary Evans Picture Library, pages 11 and 101.

Contents

To the teacher

Worksheets: language techniques

Miranda good, dad bad.

Worksheets: language into drama

Shakespeare's language

This collection of photocopiable worksheets is a response to the many requests from teachers for help with Shakespeare's language. The requests typically take the form: 'How can I help my students understand how Shakespeare's language works? What are the methods he uses to achieve his dramatic effects?'

Shakespeare's Language provides that help. It focuses directly on Shakespeare's language and how it works. It aims to enable students to understand, enjoy and use the linguistic techniques which aided Shakespeare's dramatic imagination. Each worksheet seeks to give an insight into how he wrote for the stage and how he fashioned his language for active performance – to create character, atmosphere and dramatic effect.

'You would pluck out the heart of my mystery'

Asking 'How is it done?' can kill enjoyment, just as surely as any over-analytic approach to Shakespeare. Students can enjoy Shakespeare without knowledge of many of the techniques he used. But, just as greater understanding of the skills involved in any sport deepens enjoyment of that sport, so too with Shakespeare. Knowledge about Shakespeare's use of language, a growing appreciation of his skill as a dramatist, increases enjoyment of the plays and empowers students as readers, speakers, actors and audience.

These worksheets are the outcome of the research and development work of the *Shakespeare and Schools Project*. Like all other publications in the *Cambridge School Shakespeare* series, *Shakespeare's Language* recognises that successful classroom practice assumes active rather than passive students, who are both interpreters and makers of meaning.

Teaching Shakespeare, a companion book for teachers, also published by Cambridge University Press, covers the whole range of students' experience of Shakespeare.

Knowledge about language

As a schoolboy, Shakespeare learned by heart over one hundred technical terms to describe the use of language. Nearly all of those terms have now disappeared from general use. Even Shakespeare professors do not know many of them, and today's school students certainly do not need to know such words as 'mycterismus', 'brachylogia', 'cataplexis'. Such terms get in the way of understanding and enacting the dramatic qualities of Shakespeare's language.

The headings used in the worksheets represent a basic set of terms for understanding Shakespeare's language. Most are familiar and in everyday use. Words like 'lists' or 'repetition' are preferred to older Latinate terms, and are both accurate and effective.

The worksheets in *Shakespeare's Language* are organised in two groups: 'language techniques' and 'language into drama'.

Pages 1–67 consist of worksheets on Shakespeare's language techniques: imagery, antithesis, repetition, lists, etc. These are the methods he used to achieve particular effects and can be regarded as the 'building blocks' of Shakespeare's language. This image may seem too static to describe the fluidity and subtlety of Shakespeare's dramatic construction. But in its suggestion of organisation, design and pattern, the image of 'building blocks' acknowledges Shakespeare's craftsmanship, his scrupulous artistic shaping of language.

Pages 68-143 consist of worksheets on 'language into drama', the characteristic elements of Shakespeare's plays, for example: soliloquy, dialogue, character, stories, atmosphere.

Each worksheet recognises that Shakespeare wrote scripts for performance. His language is above all else dramatic language, written to seize the imagination of an audience. The activities on each worksheet are designed to help students understand how Shakespeare's choice of language – the words, phrases, imagery and style – intensifies dramatic effect.

''Tis now the very witching time of night'

Shakespeare's theatre did not possess the sophisticated technology of stage machinery, lighting, sound effects and elaborate sets found in modern theatres. His scene painting was done through language. Words evoked tempests and sheep shearings, night or day, graveyards and battlefields, feelings of love and hate, fear and joy.

The development of Shakespeare's language

Shakespeare was essentially a man of the theatre. He was a playwright, an actor and a poet, whose genius was for intensely dramatic language. His playwriting career seems to have lasted for a little over twenty years, from about the early 1590s to somewhere around 1611. No-one can know for certain the precise date of the composition of any play. Heated arguments still take place over when he may have written particular plays, but there is general agreement about the order in which he wrote them (see page 150).

Every generalisation about Shakespeare must be treated with great caution. However, it is possible to suggest some ways in which Shakespeare's skill as a writer developed from an early play such as *Titus Andronicus*, to what was probably the final play he wrote on his own, *The Tempest*.

- A decreasing use of rhyme, and an increasing use of blank verse.
- An increasing preference for metaphor over simile.
- Less obviously 'patterned' language: verse becomes less regular, less end-stopped, making greater use of the caesura (mid-line pause).
- A move away from 'sticking to the rules' (the conventions of Elizabethan poetry and drama) to much freer, more flexible use of such conventions: for example, decreasing use of alliteration and the rhetorical devices he had learned by heart in his Stratford school room.
- Imagery becomes more organic to the play, less decorative, more condensed. Early plays give an impression of imagery being 'stuck on' as a display of ingenuity. In later plays imagery is an integral part of Shakespeare's dramatic purposes and design, as in the highly controlled use of telescoped and complex imagery in *Macbeth*.
- Decreasing lyrical use of language.
- A move away from word play for its own sake, as in the rich conceits of *Love's Labour's Lost*.
- A greater use of prose: the use of prose peaks in the middle of his career, with, for example, *Much Ado About Nothing* and *The Merry Wives of Windsor*.
- Decreasing obvious use of classical allusions.
- Fewer instances of bombastic and 'heroic' language.

Shakespeare increasingly selected, cut and restrained his early impulse to display – overtly and at length – his knowledge of how language worked. He became less inclined to put all his goods in the shop window, and more willing to leave gaps for the audience's imagination to fill. For example, in the early plays characters announce their deaths explicitly ('O I am slain'). In *Antony and Cleopatra*, Charmain's dying words are 'Ah, soldier!'

None of this is to diminish the dramatic or poetic quality of the early plays. They still make wonderful theatre.

Speaking Shakespeare

Are there rules about how Shakespeare should be spoken? Is there a 'correct way' to speak the lines? Like everything else about Shakespeare, very different answers may be given to these questions. Some would argue that there is a correct way to speak Shakespeare and that rules should be rigorously followed; others take a more relaxed approach. The two opposing views can be called 'form' and 'feeling'.

Those who believe in 'form' argue that speaking Shakespeare should make clear the metrical structure of the verse. Each line should be spoken with five stresses with a pause (however short) at the end. Learning about iambic pentameter should therefore be the first step in the study of Shakespeare's language.

The 'feeling' approach is more relaxed about rules. It argues that students should begin by speaking and acting out scenes or short extracts, to gain a sense of characters' emotions, thoughts and motivations. Students should experiment to find speaking styles appropriate to the particular dramatic situation.

In this 'feeling' view, teaching iambic pentameter comes much later. Shakespeare may well have begun his career thinking in 'line units' (in other words, a single line makes sense on its own), but he increasingly moved away from that practice, making a thought run over a line ending so that 'sense units' cease to match 'line units'. Further, to give each line five stresses becomes mechanical and unrealistic. For example, when Henry V wants to motivate his troops to attack Harfleur, the dramatic context makes it perfectly feasible that he gives his first line at least seven stresses:

/ / / / / / /
Once more into the breach, dear friends, once more.

Each teacher will decide what is suitable advice for his or her students, guided by a few commonsense suggestions:

1 Make sure you can be heard by your 'audience', who might be only one other student, a small group, the whole class, or a large audience watching a school play.
2 Accent is immaterial. Don't put on an artificial, false voice, but use your own natural voice. Shakespeare does not have to be spoken in the Received Pronounciation of the English upper middle classes. A Shakespeare king does not have any particular accent, but he usually speaks with the tone of authority.
3 Look for the 'sense units' in the language, which will sometimes be shorter than one line, sometimes longer, and sometimes the line itself. When you speak as a character, try to communicate his or her thoughts and feelings in an appropriate tone and style.
4 Pause or emphasise whenever you think it seems appropriate for dramatic effect, to give significance to what you are saying. Silence can be very powerful.
5 There is never one single 'right' delivery: any speech may be spoken in many ways. The accepted style of speaking and performing Shakespeare changes from generation to generation.
6 Remember that Shakespeare wrote plays, not recitation pieces. His language is an invitation to imaginative, dramatic enactment.

How to use the worksheets

The worksheets can be used in many different ways to deepen students' knowledge and enjoyment of Shakespeare's language. Teachers can choose to construct their own course, selecting worksheets suitable to their particular students' needs and interests.

Here are some suggestions for ways to use the worksheets:

1. As a series of lessons on Shakespeare's language. For example, an eight-lesson course which covers major features: antithesis, imagery, lists, repetition, verse, prose, songs, rhyme.
2. To enrich study of a particular play. Here, worksheets are used at appropriate points to help students' understanding of an aspect of the play being studied, for example: soliloquy, persuasion, theme, etc. The worksheets contain an explanation of the particular feature, as well as comparative extracts from other plays. (The index of extracts on pages 146–148 indicates the precise source of each extract. The index of plays on page 149 lists each play and its relevant worksheets.)
3. As a series of lessons on 'stories', 'atmosphere', 'characters', etc.
4. As stimulus lessons, using the extracts for active introductions to Shakespeare.

Two worksheets form a unit of work for a single lesson. The boxed reference at the top left-hand corner of each sheet indicates which sheets go together. The first worksheet gives an introduction to the feature of language to be studied. The accompanying worksheet provides an extract for active study through speaking, enacting, creating a context, and other methods. Because this is dramatic speech, written to be spoken in performance, even a few lines contain many opportunities for imaginative exploration, as well as offering students a range of opportunities for inference and speculation.

Occasionally only one worksheet is needed.

A worksheet often contains several activities, to give students a range of options. Sometimes, teachers may ask all students to work on the same activity.

It is vital that students enact the extracts, speaking them aloud to experience for themselves the distinctive emotional rhythms of the language. Such active experience of its dramatic power gives students that sense of ownership that is the key to successful learning.

By close study of one feature of Shakespeare's language, students achieve mastery of that particular element, and a growing appreciation of the interconnectedness of every aspect of Shakespeare's language in heightening dramatic effect.

Imagery

USE WITH ONE OF PAGES 2 TO 11

Imagery is the use of emotionally charged words and phrases which conjure up vivid mental pictures in the imagination. King Lear, waking from his madness and seeing his daughter Cordelia, expresses his suffering in powerful imagery:

> You do me wrong to take me out o'th'grave.
> Thou art a soul in bliss, but I am bound
> Upon a wheel of fire, that mine own tears
> Do scald like molten lead.

Such images play a key part in every Shakespeare play. They are a kind of verbal scene painting which appeals to the emotions. They deepen and intensify imaginative and dramatic impact, giving insight into characters' feelings and thoughts:

> O, full of scorpions is my mind, dear wife!

In each play, clusters of repeated images build up a sense of the themes of the play. Examples are the images of false appearance in *Macbeth*: ('Look like the innocent flower, but be the serpent under it'); of light and darkness in *Romeo and Juliet*; the imagery of torture, fracture and suffering in *King Lear*.

In every play Shakespeare uses imagery from nature: sun, moon and stars; the seasons; the sea; animals and birds and so on. The bear baiting he saw near the Globe Theatre gave him a key image for Macbeth, surrounded by his enemies, and facing death:

> They have tied me to a stake, I cannot fly,
> But bear-like I must fight the course

Metaphor and simile: All Shakespeare's imagery uses metaphor or simile.

A simile compares one thing to another using 'like' or 'as':

> Death lies on her like an untimely frost.

A metaphor is also a comparison. It does not use 'like' or 'as' but suggests that two dissimilar things are actually the same:

> There's daggers in men's smiles

---

1. Pick out some of the imagery on the accompanying worksheet, or in the play you are currently studying. Identify which are similes and which are metaphors. Use one or more images to design a poster advertising a production of the play.

2. In the Zeffirelli film of *Hamlet*, as Hamlet speaks the 'To be, or not to be' soliloquy, the camera slowly pans around a burial vault, illustrating the imagery of the speech with appropriate pictures (skulls and bones, etc.). In Polanski's film of Mac*beth*, a bear-baiting post is used at several points in the play to emphasise the bear-baiting image.

   Prepare a camera 'shooting script' for the lines on the accompanying worksheet to suggest how you would illustrate the imagery in a film.

Imagery: the king as the sun

USE WITH PAGE 1

King Richard II compares himself to the sun whose light exposes all criminals.

Discomfortable cousin, knowest thou not
That when the searching eye of heaven is hid
Behind the globe and lights the lower world
Then thieves and robbers range abroad unseen
In murders and in outrage boldly here.
But when from under this terrestrial ball
He fires the proud tops of the eastern pines
And darts his light through every guilty hole
Then murders, treasons and detested sins,
The cloak of night being plucked from off their backs,
Stand bare and naked, trembling at themselves?
So when this thief, this traitor, Bullingbrook,
Who all this while hath revelled in the night
Whilst we were wandering with the antipodes
Shall see us rising in our throne the east
His treasons will sit blushing in his face,
Not able to endure the sight of day,
But self-affrighted tremble at his sin.
Not all the water in the rough rude sea
Can wash the balm off from an anointed king.
The breath of worldly men cannot depose
The deputy elected by the Lord.

terrestrial ball
the earth

Bullingbrook
King Richard's cousin, who challenges him

antipodes
opposite side of the earth

anointed
marked with holy oil ('balm') to show rightful kingship

deputy
rightful king

1 Explore ways of speaking and acting out the lines to make the imagery as clear as possible to an audience.

2 After the extended imagery of the king as the sun, in the final four lines Richard uses two different images. Suggest which you find most imaginatively powerful, then make up four further lines containing an image of your own.

3 See also Activities 1 and 2 on page 1.

Imagery: the horrors of civil war

USE WITH PAGE 1

Julius Caesar has been assassinated. Over Caesar's dead body, Mark Antony prophesies horrific civil war.

cumber
trouble or load down

fell
cruel, savage

Ate (pronounced Artee)
the fanatical goddess of revenge and mischief

carrion
nearly dead, food for wild beasts

O, pardon me, thou bleeding piece of earth,
That I am meek and gentle with these butchers!
Thou art the ruins of the noblest man
That ever livèd in the tide of times.
Woe to the hand that shed this costly blood!
Over thy wounds now do I prophesy –
Which like dumb mouths do ope their ruby lips
To beg the voice and utterance of my tongue –
A curse shall light upon the limbs of men:
Domestic fury and fierce civil strife
Shall cumber all the parts of Italy;
Blood and destruction shall be so in use
And dreadful objects so familiar
That mothers shall but smile when they behold
Their infants quartered with the hands of war,
All pity choked with custom of fell deeds;
And Caesar's spirit, ranging for revenge,
With Ate by his side come hot from hell,
Shall in these confines with a monarch's voice
Cry havoc and let slip the dogs of war,
That this foul deed shall smell above the earth
With carrion men groaning for burial.

1 Almost every line contains an image ('bleeding piece of earth', 'butchers', 'ruins', etc.). Identify as many images as you can, then make a list of them in the order that you find most imaginatively powerful. Compare your list with those of other students.

2 'The dogs of war' has often been used as a newspaper headline in times of conflict. Make up a newspaper page in which each item or picture has a headline or caption taken from the imagery of these lines.

3 Experiment with different ways of speaking Antony's lines. For example, whisper them, speak them calmly and rationally, as a solemn ritual, etc. Find a style that you feel is appropriate to a stage delivery.

4 See also Activities 1 and 2 on page 1.

Imagery: the futility of life

USE WITH PAGE 1

Macbeth, besieged by his enemies, has just been told of the death of his wife.

Tomorrow, and tomorrow, and tomorrow
Creeps in this petty pace from day to day
To the last syllable of recorded time;
And all our yesterdays have lighted fools
The way to dusty death. Out, out, brief candle,
Life's but a walking shadow, a poor player
That struts and frets his hour upon the stage
And then is heard no more. It is a tale
Told by an idiot, full of sound and fury
Signifying nothing.

1 Explore different ways of speaking the lines (sadly, angrily, fearfully, wonderingly, etc.).

2 Share out the lines and devise a choral-speaking presentation with accompanying actions.

3 Select short phrases (for example, 'brief candle'). Imagine they are book titles. Write the first sentence for each book.

4 See also Activities 1 and 2 on page 1.

Imagery: acting and theatre

USE WITH PAGE 1

In *The Tempest,* Prospero compares the brevity of human life and achievement with the impermanence of theatre and acting. Just as actors vanish into thin air, so too will everyone and everything.

baseless fabric
flimsy structure

all which it inherit
all who live there now and later

rack
clouds painted on scenery

Our revels now are ended; these our actors,
As I foretold you, were all spirits, and
Are melted into air, into thin air;
And like the baseless fabric of this vision,
The cloud-capped towers, the gorgeous palaces,
The solemn temples, the great globe itself,
Yea, all which it inherit, shall dissolve,
And like this insubstantial pageant faded
Leave not a rack behind. We are such stuff
As dreams are made on; and our little life
Is rounded with a sleep.

'The great globe itself'.
The image suggests both Shakespeare's Globe theatre and the world itself.

1 Prospero's lines have become famous as a metaphor for the impermanence of human life. Work out how they might be spoken on stage. Suggest his tone of voice, which words he might emphasise, where he might pause.

2 Devise a choral-speaking presentation of the lines in which several voices speak together. Use repetitions, echoes, together with movement and other dramatic action to accompany the voices.

3 See also Activities 1 and 2 on page 1.

Imagery: society as a beehive

USE WITH PAGE 1

In *King Henry V*, the Archbishop of Canterbury compares human society to a colony of honey bees.

diverse
many

endeavour
human activity

butt
target

Make boot
plunder

executors
executioners

full reference/To one consent
fully agreed on a single purpose

contrariously
in opposite ways

dial's
sundial's

Therefore doth heaven divide
The state of man in diverse functions,
Setting endeavour in continual motion,
To which is fixèd as an aim or butt
Obedience. For so work the honey bees,
Creatures that by a rule in nature teach
The act of order to a peopled kingdom.
They have a king, and officers of sorts,
Where some like magistrates correct at home,
Others like merchants venture trade abroad,
Others like soldiers, armèd in their stings,
Make boot upon the summer's velvet buds,
Which pillage they with merry march bring home
To the tent royal of their emperor,
Who, busied in his majesties, surveys
The singing masons building roofs of gold,
The civil citizens kneading up the honey,
The poor mechanic porters crowding in
Their heavy burdens at his narrow gate,
The sad-eyed justice with his surly hum
Delivering o'er to executors pale
The lazy yawning drone. I this infer,
That many things, having full reference
To one consent, may work contrariously.
As many arrows loosèd several ways
Come to one mark; as many ways meet in one town,
As many fresh streams meet in one salt sea,
As many lines close in the dial's centre,
So may a thousand actions, once afoot
End in one purpose, and be all well borne
Without defeat.

1. In groups, one person reads the lines aloud, while the other members of the group mime each action mentioned.
2. In the final nine lines, another set of images is given. Identify each, and make up several more to illustrate Canterbury's argument.
3. Co-operation or dominance? Is the image of a beehive as a model of human society appropriate, or a false, misleading comparison? Take sides and argue for and against the harmonious society of both bees and humans that the lines present.
4. See also Activities 1 and 2 on page 1.

Imagery: opening Twelfth Night

USE WITH PAGE 1

Twelfth Night begins with Orsino calling for music to feed his hunger for love.

surfeiting
over-filled

That strain again
play that again

validity and pitch
high value

falls into abatement
is lessened

fancy
love

high fantastical
intensely imaginative

hart
male deer

pestilence
plague

fell
savage

ORSINO If music be the food of love, play on;
Give me excess of it, that surfeiting,
The appetite may sicken and so die.
That strain again, it had a dying fall;
O it came o'er my ear like the sweet sound
That breathes upon a bank of violets,
Stealing and giving odour. Enough; no more.
'Tis not so sweet now as it was before.
O spirit of love, how quick and fresh art thou,
That, not withstanding thy capacity,
Receiveth as the sea. Nought enters there,
Of what validity and pitch soe'er,
But falls into abatement and low price
Even in a minute. So full of shapes is fancy,
That it alone is high fantastical.
CURIO Will you go hunt, my lord?
ORSINO What, Curio?
CURIO The hart.
ORSINO Why so I do, the noblest that I have.
O when mine eyes did see Olivia first,
Methought she purged the air of pestilence;
That instant was I turned into a hart,
And my desires like fell and cruel hounds
E'er since pursue me.

1 Imagine you are about to stage *Twelfth Night*. You wish to give the audience as vivid an experience as possible of the imagery in these opening lines (music, flower scent, sea, hunting). You can use design, sound lighting, props, etc. Work out in detail how you will stage the lines – then act out your version.

2 See also Activities 1 and 2 on page 1.

Imagery: Macbeth and Malcolm

USE WITH PAGE 1

As the thanes (Scottish noblemen) march to besiege Macbeth in Dunsinane castle, they describe Macbeth, the tyrant, and Malcolm, who seeks to overthrow him.

the tyrant
(Macbeth)

distempered cause
corrupt dictatorship

Now minutely ... faith-breach
every minute there's a rebellion protesting about his treachery

pestered senses
troubled conscience

start
panic

the med'cine of the sickly weal
the cure of the diseased kingdom (Malcolm)

purge
cure by cleansing

MENTEITH What does the tyrant?
CAITHNESS Great Dunsinane he strongly fortifies.
Some say he's mad; others that lesser hate him
Do call it valiant fury, but for certain
He cannot buckle his distempered cause
Within the belt of rule.
ANGUS Now does he feel
His secret murders sticking on his hands.
Now minutely revolts upbraid his faith-breach;
Those he commands, move only in command,
Nothing in love. Now does he feel his title
Hang loose about him, like a giant's robe
Upon a dwarfish thief.
MENTEITH Who then shall blame
His pestered senses to recoil and start,
When all that is within him does condemn
Itself for being there?
CAITHNESS Well, march we on
To give obedience where 'tis truly owed
Meet we the med'cine of the sickly weal,
And with him pour we in our country's purge,
Each drop of us.
LENNOX Or so much as it needs
To dew the sovereign flower and drown the weeds.
Make we our march towards Birnam.

Exeunt, marching

1. In groups, three students speak the lines, pausing at each punctuation mark. In the pauses, others in the group act out the descriptions of Macbeth and Malcolm.
2. Find an appropriate way of illustrating, either by acting or through artwork, the imagery used to describe Macbeth (first fifteen lines), and Malcolm (final seven lines).
3. See also Activities 1 and 2 on page 1.

Imagery: England as a garden

USE WITH PAGE 1

The gardeners in *King Richard II* use the image of England as a neglected garden. The image suggests that just as a neglected garden becomes full of weeds and pests, so England, when the king neglects his duties, becomes disordered and overrun with quarrels between ambitious, self-seeking courtiers.

noisome
harmful

in the compass of a pale
within the limits of a fence

firm estate
strong environment

knots
patterned flower beds

He that hath suffered
King Richard who allowed

Bullingbrook
King Richard's cousin

GARDENER Go thou, and like an executioner
Cut off the heads of too-fast-growing sprays
That look too lofty in our commonwealth.
All must be even in our government.
You thus employed, I will go root away
The noisome weeds which without profit suck
The soil's fertility from wholesome flowers.
SERVANT Why should we, in the compass of a pale,
Keep law and form and due proportion,
Showing as in a model our firm estate,
When our sea-wallèd garden, the whole land,
Is full of weeds, her fairest flowers choked up,
Her fruit trees all unpruned, her hedges ruined,
Her knots disordered and her wholesome herbs
Swarming with caterpillars?
GARDENER Hold thy peace.
He that hath suffered this disordered spring
Hath now himself met with the fall of leaf.
The weeds which his broad spreading leaves did shelter,
That seemed in eating him to hold him up,
Are plucked up root and all by Bullingbrook.

1 Experiment with different ways of speaking the lines. Think particularly about whether the gardeners would use a country dialect, or some other accent.

2 Design costumes for the corrupt courtiers who elsewhere in the play are called 'the caterpillars of the commonwealth'.

3 Use the imagery as inspiration for a poem or short report on some aspect of present-day society.

4 See also Activities 1 and 2 on page 1.

Imagery: a miscellany

USE WITH PAGE 1

I have supped full with horrors

scarf up the tender eye of pitiful day

My intents are savage-wild
More fierce and more inexorable far
Than empty tigers or the roaring sea

Whiter than new snow upon a raven's back

The slings and arrows of outrageous fortune

O my offence is rank, it smells to heaven

Why what's the matter,
That you have such a February face,
So full of frost, of storm, and cloudiness

Death lies on her like an untimely frost

They'll take suggestion as a cat laps milk

The moon, like to a silver bow
New bent in heaven

Humanity must perforce prey on itself
Like monsters of the deep

How sharper than a serpent's tooth it is
To have a thankless child

The quality of mercy is not strained
It droppeth as the gentle rain from heaven

O serpent heart, hid with a flow'ring face!

Thou art a boil,
A plague-sore, or embossèd carbuncle
In my corrupted blood

She sat like Patience on a monument
Smiling at grief.

1 Make up a staged presentation of some of the images so that it presents a coherent story.

2 Illustrate a selection of the images in a method of your choice. For example, 'the dogs of war' has often been used as a newspaper headline in time of conflict. Make up a newspaper page in which each item or picture has a headline or caption taken from the imagery of these lines.

3 See also Activities 1 and 2 on page 1.

Imagery: personification

USE WITH PAGE 1

Shakespeare often uses personification: turning all kinds of things (death, time, war, love, England, etc.) into persons, giving them human feelings and attributes. For example, Malcolm speaks of Scotland's suffering under Macbeth:

I think our country sinks beneath the yoke;
It weeps, it bleeds, and each new day a gash
Is added to her wounds.

In *King John*, Constance, in her grief for her son, longs for death.

No, I defy all counsel, all redress,
But that which ends all counsel, true redress:
Death! Death, O amiable, lovely Death,
Thou odoriferous stench, sound rottenness,
Arise forth from the couch of lasting night,
Thou hate and terror to prosperity,
And I will kiss thy detestable bones,
And put my eyeballs in thy vaulty brows,
And ring these fingers with thy household worms,
And stop this gap of breath with fulsome dust,
And be a carrion monster like thyself.
Come, grin on me, and I will think thou smil'st,
And buss thee as thy wife. Misery's love,
O come to me!

redress
compensation, consolation

odoriferous stench
fragrant stink

vaulty
empty

household
familiar

fulsome
nauseating, foul

carrion
corpse-eating

buss
kiss

1. How far do you feel this medieval woodcut matches Constance's description? Speak the lines with this image in mind.
2. Experiment with ways of dramatising Constance's lines. For example, begin by speaking them as a kind of prayer, emphasising every 'And'.
3. Make up six or more lines of your own that personify love, war, a country or an emotion.
4. See also Activities 1 and 2 on page 1.

Antithesis 1

USE WITH PAGE 13

Every Shakespeare play makes frequent use of antithesis: the opposition of words or phrases against each other:

> To be, or not to be ...

'To be' is the thesis, 'not to be' is the antithesis.

Shakespeare knew that the essence of drama is conflict. His plays depict conflict at every level. In the history plays there are bloody struggles for the throne. In the comedies, the course of true love never runs smooth, beset by all kinds of mishaps, mistakes and quarrels. In the tragedies, good and evil oppose each other.

Shakespeare's language expresses conflict in the use of antithesis. Just as character is set against character (Hamlet versus Claudius, Iago versus Othello), so Shakespeare sets the word against the word:

> For night owls shriek where mounting larks should sing

'night owls' against 'mounting larks', 'shriek' against 'sing'

To sue to live, I find I seek to die

And nothing is, but what is not

Fair is foul, and foul is fair

Cannot be ill, cannot be good

My only love sprung from my only hate!

My grave is like to be my wedding bed

1 a Speak aloud the examples on page 13. To discover the see-sawing, conflicting movement of the language, weigh out each antithesis as if your hands were a pair of scales.

b Work with a partner, link hands and gently push and pull as you speak the lines to each other. Experiment with different movements to discover how the antitheses give the language a physical, to and fro, opposing movement.

2 In a group, prepare a choral-speaking version of Sonnet 66. Add actions to show as many of the antitheses as you can.

Antithesis 2

USE WITH PAGE 12

In *Coriolanus*, the patrician (upper class) Coriolanus makes much use of antithesis as he contemptuously scorns the ordinary people of Rome, the plebeians:

> What would you have, you curs,
> That like not peace nor war? The one affrights you,
> The other makes you proud. He that trusts to you,
> Where he should find you lions, finds you hares,
> Where foxes, geese. You are no surer, no,
> Than is the coal of fire upon the ice,
> Or hailstone in the sun. Your virtue is
> To make him worthy whose offence subdues him,
> And curse that justice did it. Who deserves greatness
> Deserves your hate.

peace	**affrights**	**lions**	**foxes**
war	**proud**	**hares**	**geese**
fire	**hailstone**	**worthy**	**greatness**
ice	**sun**	**subdues**	**hate**

In Sonnet 66 Shakespeare lists the injustices that make him long for 'restful death'. Each of the first twelve lines contains at least one antithesis.

As to behold for example to see

desert a deserving person, justice

gilded honour noble dignity

strumpeted made a prostitute

limping sway weak government

doctor-like like a pompous and ignorant teacher

simplicity stupidity

> Tired with all these, for restful death I cry:
> As to behold desert a beggar born,
> And needy nothing trimmed in jollity,
> And purest faith unhappily forsworn,
> And gilded honour shamefully misplaced,
> And maiden virtue rudely strumpeted,
> And right perfection wrongfully disgraced,
> And strength by limping sway disablèd,
> And art made tongue-tied by authority,
> And folly (doctor-like) controlling skill,
> And simple truth miscalled simplicity,
> And captive good attending captain ill:
> Tired with all these, from these would I be gone,
> Save that to die, I leave my love alone.

Repetition

USE WITH ONE OF PAGES 15 TO 21

Shakespeare's use of repetition gives his language great dramatic force. Repeated words, phrases, rhythms and word sounds (rhyme, alliteration, assonance) add to the emotional intensity of a moment or scene, heightening serious or comic effect.

Early in his playwriting career Shakespeare made much use of repetition in fairly obvious ways. *Richard III* is full of examples of highly patterned repetition:

> Was ever woman in this humour woo'ed?
> Was ever woman in this humour won?
>
> Where is thy husband now? Where be thy brothers?
> Where be thy two sons? Wherein dost thou joy?
> Who sues, and kneels and says 'God save the Queen'?
> Where be the bending peers that flattered thee?
> Where be the thronging troops that followed thee?

Repeating a single word can deepen irony. For example in *Julius Caesar* Antony constantly repeats 'honourable' in his Forum speech when he means quite the opposite. Repetition can also heighten comedy, as when Petruchio teases Katherina in *The Taming of the Shrew*:

> PETRUCHIO Good morrow, Kate, for that's your name, I hear.
> KATHERINA Well have you heard, but something hard of hearing –
> They call me Katherine that do talk of me.
> PETRUCHIO You lie, in faith, for you are called plain Kate,
> And bonny Kate, and sometimes Kate the curst.
> But Kate, the prettiest Kate in Christendom,
> Kate of Kate-Hall, my super-dainty Kate –
> For dainties are all Kates – and therefore, Kate,
> Take this of me, Kate of my consolation:

Shakespeare also knew that a single repeated word can be deeply moving. At the end of *King Lear*, Lear grieves over the dead body of his cruelly murdered daughter Cordelia:

> Thou'lt come no more,
> Never, never, never, never, never.

1 Turn at random to any page of the play you are currently studying (or to the accompanying worksheet). Identify all the ways in which Shakespeare uses repetition on that page. Suggest how actors might use those repetitions to increase dramatic effect.

2 Work in pairs and experiment with ways of speaking Petruchio's and Kate's lines above to increase comic effect.

Repetition: parody

USE WITH PAGE 14

Parody is a mocking imitation of a writer's style. Shakespeare parodies the use of repetition in *A Midsummer Night's Dream* as Bottom begins the play within the play that he will perform with his fellow workmen:

O grim-looked night, O night with hue so black,
O night which ever art when day is not!
O night, O night, alack, alack, alack,
I fear my Thisbe's promise is forgot!
And thou, O wall, O sweet, O lovely wall,
That stand'st between her father's ground and mine,
Thou wall, O wall, O sweet and lovely wall,
Show me thy chink, to blink through with mine eyne.

1 Speak Bottom's lines emphasising all the repetitions of words, sounds, phrases and so on. Add actions that you feel are appropriate.

2 Write and perform your own parody of one of Shakespeare's scenes or characters. Use as much repetition as you can, in a style similar to Bottom's speech.

Repetition: a shepherd's life

USE WITH PAGE 14

In *King Henry VI* part 3 the battle of Towton rages. King Henry sits on a molehill and thinks how much happier he would be as a shepherd.

homely swain
ordinary shepherd

dials
sundials

ewes
female sheep

poor fools
innocent creatures

ean
bear lambs

O God! Methinks it were a happy life
To be no better than a homely swain;
To sit upon a hill, as I do now;
To carve out dials quaintly, point by point,
Thereby to see the minutes how they run:
How many makes the hour full complete,
How many hours brings about the day,
How many days will finish up the year,
How many years a mortal man may live.
When this is known, then to divide the times:
So many hours must I tend my flock,
So many hours must I take my rest,
So many hours must I contemplate,
So many hours must I sport myself,
So many days my ewes have been with young,
So many weeks ere the poor fools will ean,
So many years ere I shall shear the fleece.
So minutes, hours, days, months, and years,
Passed over to the end they were created,
Would bring white hairs unto a quiet grave.

1 Explore ways of speaking the lines to emphasise the repetitions. Then see if you can speak them in a conversational style, playing down the repetitions. Decide on an appropriate mood and style of how they might be spoken on stage.

2 Write a piece in praise of an occupation that seems to you to have particularly attractive features. Use the lines above as a model.

Repetition: an appeal for justice

USE WITH PAGE 14

In *Measure for Measure* Isabella calls for justice against the corrupt Angelo who has used his position of power to blackmail her.

redress
justice

suitor
petitioner, supplicant

Cut off
executed

forsworn
perjured (a liar under oath)

reck'ning
time

ISABELLA Justice, justice, justice, justice!
DUKE Relate your wrongs: in what? By whom? Be brief.
Here is Lord Angelo shall give you justice;
Reveal yourself to him.
ISABELLA Oh worthy Duke,
You bid me seek redemption of the devil.
Hear me yourself: for that which I must speak
Must either punish me, not being believed,
Or wring redress from you. Hear me, oh hear me, here!
ANGELO My Lord, her wits I fear me are not firm;
She hath been a suitor to me for her brother
Cut off by course of justice.
ISABELLA By course of justice!
ANGELO And she will speak most bitterly and strange.
ISABELLA Most strange, but yet most truly will I speak.
That Angelo's forsworn, is it not strange?
That Angelo's a murderer, is't not strange?
That Angelo is an adulterous thief,
An hypocrite, a virgin-violator,
Is it not strange, and strange?
DUKE Nay, it is ten times strange.
ISABELLA It is not truer he is Angelo
Than this is all as true as it is strange;
Nay, it is ten times true, for truth is truth
To th'end of reck'ning.

1 Take parts as Isabella, the Duke, and Angelo. Play the lines emphasising the ritual of the various repetitions. Then explore other ways of speaking and staging them.

2 Write detailed notes on the lines for the guidance of actors, including advice on how the different repetitions can deepen dramatic effect.

Repetition: giving away a throne

USE WITH PAGE 14

Richard II resigns all the symbols and powers of kingship to his cousin Henry Bullingbrook.

undo myself
resign my kingship

sway
power

balm
anointing oil

acts, decrees, and statues
laws

Now, mark me how I will undo myself.
I give this heavy weight from off my head
And this unwieldy sceptre from my hand,
The pride of kingly sway from out my heart.
With mine own tears I wash away my balm;
With mine own hands I give away my crown;
With mine own tongue deny my sacred state;
With mine own breath release all duteous oaths.
All pomp and majesty I do forswear;
My manors, rents, revenues I forgo;
My acts, decrees, and statutes I deny.
God pardon all oaths that are broke to me;
God keep all vows unbroke are made to thee.
Make me that nothing have with nothing grieved,
And thou with all pleased that hast all achieved.
Long mayst thou live in Richard's seat to sit,
And soon lie Richard in an earthy pit.
God save King Henry, unkinged Richard says,
And send him many years of sunshine days.

1 Handing over kingship is an intensely serious occasion, carried out with great ritual. Here, Shakespeare builds that ritual into the repeated rhythms of the language. Invent a ceremony to accompany the words, with repetitive, formal actions to match the language.

2 Write a parody of Richard's language to be spoken on the day you cease to be a school or college student.

Repetition: echoes

USE WITH PAGE 14

In *The Merchant of Venice* Bassanio tries to explain why he gave away Portia's ring, but Portia mockingly echoes his excuse.

conceive
understand, imagine

abate
lessen

contain
keep secure

BASSANIO Sweet Portia,
If you did know to whom I gave the ring,
If you did know for whom I gave the ring,
And would conceive for what I gave the ring,
And how unwillingly I left the ring,
When naught would be accepted but the ring,
You would abate the strength of your displeasure.
PORTIA If you had known the virtue of the ring,
Or half her worthiness that gave the ring,
Or your own honour to contain the ring,
You would not then have parted with the ring.

In *All's Well That Ends Well* Diana mocks Bertram's language in order to obtain his ring.

'longing
belonging

obloquy
disgrace

bid
ruled

DIANA Give me that ring.
BERTRAM I'll lend it thee, my dear; but have no power
To give it from me.
DIANA Will you not, my lord?
BERTRAM It is an honour 'longing to our house,
Bequeathèd down from many ancestors,
Which were the greatest obloquy i'th'world
In me to lose.
DIANA Mine honour's such a ring,
My chastity's the jewel of our house,
Bequeathèd down from many ancestors,
Which were the greatest obloquy i'th'world
In me to lose. Thus your own proper wisdom
Brings in the champion Honour on my part,
Against your vain assault.
BERTRAM Here, take my ring!
My house, mine honour, yea, my life, be thine,
And I'll be bid by thee.

1 Take parts and speak both extracts. Discuss the similarities and differences of the repetition.

2 Write a short dialogue between two characters in which one mockingly echoes the language of the other.

Repetition: fevered obsessions

USE WITH PAGE 14

In *The Winter's Tale*, Leontes, King of Sicilia, believes (wrongly) that his wife is having an affair with his best friend Polixenes, King of Bohemia. He is maddened with jealousy.

Is whispering nothing?
Is leaning cheek to cheek? Is meeting noses?
Kissing with inside lip? Stopping the career
Of laughter with a sigh? – a note infallible
Of breaking honesty – Horsing foot on foot?
Skulking in corners? Wishing clocks more swift?
Hours, minutes? Noon, midnight? And all eyes
Blind with the pin and web but theirs – theirs only,
That would unseen be wicked? Is this nothing?
Why then the world and all that's in't is nothing,
The covering sky is nothing, Bohemia nothing,
My wife is nothing, nor nothing have these nothings,
If this be nothing.

note infallible
absolutely certain sign

Horsing
touching (playing footsy)

pin and web
cataracts (diseases of the eye)

Bohemia
(Polixenes, King of Bohemia, Leontes' best friend)

In *Timon of Athens*, Timon has been driven to hatred of all humankind by the ingratitude of those people he once believed to be his friends. He tells three bandits that everything and everyone is a thief:

The sun's a thief, and with his great attraction
Robs the vast sea. The moon's an arrant thief,
And her pale fire she snatches from the sun.
The sea's a thief, whose liquid surge resolves
The moon into salt tears. The earth's a thief,
That feeds and breeds by a composture stol'n
From general excrement. Each thing's a thief.
The laws, your curb and whip, in their rough power
Has left unchecked theft. Love not yourselves. Away!
Rob one another. There's more gold. Cut throats,
All that you meet are thieves.

arrant
notorious, out-and-out

composture stol'n From general excrement
compost made from decay of all things

your curb and whip
that restrains and punishes you

left unchecked
failed to prevent

Leontes is obsessed with jealousy, Timon with misanthropy (hatred of humankind). Pick out all the ways in which different kinds of repetition intensify the emotional impact of each speech. Experiment with ways of delivering the lines to convey the deranged state of each character's mind.

Repetition: sounds

USE WITH PAGE 14

Alliteration is the repetition of consonants, usually at the beginning of words. In *Twelfth Night* the entrance of the foolish Sir Andrew Aguecheek is greeted with:

More matter for a May morning!

Assonance is the repetition of vowel sounds. In *King John*, Shakespeare gives Lewis the Dauphin a tongue-twister, full of assonance as it squeezes seven repetitions of the same sound into one line:

What lusty trumpet thus doth summon us?

Shakespeare knew that a pattern of repeated sounds offers opportunities to actors to intensify emotional impact. In *Macbeth*, the witches combine assonance with alliteration to hypnotic effect:

Thrice to thine, and thrice to mine,
And thrice again, to make up nine.

Shakespeare was not afraid to poke fun at language. In A Midsummer Night's Dream he puts words into the mouth of Quince to mock poet-playwrights who took alliteration too seriously:

Whereat with blade, with bloody, blameful blade,
He bravely broached his boiling bloody breast.

Onomatopoeia is the use of words whose sounds mimic what they describe. At the end of *The Tempest*, the Boatswain speaks of 'roaring, shrieking, howling, jingling chains'. In *King Lear*, Edgar conjures up the sounds of the sea-shore:

The murmuring surge,
That on th'unnumbered idle pebble chafes

1 Identify six or seven examples of alliteration and assonance in the Shakespeare play you are currently studying. Suggest how the actor might speak each example to heighten dramatic effect.

2 Newspapers and magazines often use alliteration and assonance in headlines. Imagine you are a sub-editor on a show business paper which specialises in alliterative headlines. Invent six or seven headlines for reviews of Shakespeare plays (for example, 'Denmark's Dangerous Dane Delays Delightfully').

3 Write a short poem or paragraph on 'Should students study Shakespeare?' using as much alliteration, assonance and onomatopoeia of your own as possible.

Lists

USE WITH ONE OF PAGES 23 TO 27

One of Shakespeare's favourite methods with language was to accumulate words or phrases rather like a list. He knew that such 'piling up' of language can increase dramatic effect and express some vital aspect of the play by intensifying description, atmosphere or argument. For example, Macbeth's character is vividly summed up by Malcolm:

grant admit
Luxurious lustful
Sudden violent

I grant him bloody,
Luxurious, avaricious, false, deceitful,
Sudden, malicious, smacking of every sin
That has a name.

Richard III's mother describes her son:

Techy irritable
age confirmed maturity
subtle cunning

Techy and wayward was thy infancy;
Thy schooldays, frightful, desperate, wild and furious;
Thy prime of manhood, daring, bold and venturous
Thy age confirmed, proud, subtle, sly and bloody.

Shylock in *The Merchant of Venice* insists on his humanity, and his list adds compelling force to his argument:

Hath not a Jew eyes? Hath not a Jew hands, organs, dimensions, senses, affections, passions? Fed with the same food, hurt with the same weapons, subject to the same diseases, healed by the same means, warmed and cooled by the same winter and summer as a Christian is?

A list of names of the French nobility killed at the Battle of Agincourt, creates an impression of a medieval world of chivalry in *King Henry V*:

Charles Delabret, High Constable of France;
Jacques of Châtillon, Admiral of France,
The master of the Crossbow, Lord Rambures;
John, Duke of Alençon, Antony, Duke of Brabant
The brother to the Duke of Burgundy …

1 Speak each of the lists above in a style which you think is appropriate. Try to give each item its own special emphasis or tone, to make it distinctive and memorable.

2 Act out the description of Macbeth above, showing in a brief mime or drama each of his qualities. There are at least eight characteristics – or fourteen if you act out the seven deadly sins!

3 Identify as many lists as you can in the play you are currently studying (a list may be as short as three or four items). Select several and act them out.

4 Experiment with changing the order of words in some of the lists. Suggest why you think Shakespeare decided that the order he chose was the most dramatically effective.

Lists: the witches' cauldron

USE WITH PAGE 22

The three witches in *Macbeth* prepare a revolting stew.

brindled
striped with colour

hedge-pig
hedgehog

Harpier
a familiar (a demon who helped witches)

Sweltered venom
poisonous sweat

Blind-worm
slow-worm

howlet
young owl

FIRST WITCH Thrice the brindled cat hath mewed.
SECOND WITCH Thrice and once the hedge-pig whined.
THIRD WITCH Harpier cries, ''Tis time, 'tis time.'
FIRST WITCH Round about the cauldron go;
In the poisoned entrails throw.
Toad, that under cold stone
Days and nights has thirty-one
Sweltered venom sleeping got,
Boil thou first i'th'charmèd pot.
ALL Double, double toil and trouble;
Fire burn, and cauldron bubble.
SECOND WITCH Fillet of a fenny snake,
In the cauldron boil and bake:
Eye of newt, and toe of frog,
Wool of bat, and tongue of dog,
Adder's fork, and blind-worm's sting,
Lizard's leg, and howlet's wing,
For a charm of powerful trouble,
Like a hell-broth, boil and bubble.
ALL Double, double toil and trouble;
Fire burn, and cauldron bubble.

1 Share the lines between you, get stirring, and you'll find the witches' language is easy to learn by heart!

2 Make up your own list of ingredients: they can be as revolting as the witches', or you may wish to brew up a wholesome, healthy brew with 'good' ingredients.

Lists: things I'd rather do

USE WITH PAGE 22

In *Much Ado About Nothing* Benedick tells the Prince, his commander, all the things he would rather do than meet Beatrice:

> Will your grace command me any service to the world's end? I will go on the slightest errand now to the Antipodes that you can devise to send me on: I will fetch you a tooth-picker now from the furthest inch of Asia: bring you the length of Prester John's foot: fetch you a hair off the great Cham's beard: do you any embassage to the Pygmies, rather than hold three words conference with this Harpy.

Antipodes
opposite side of the earth

Prester John
legendary Christian king in Africa or Asia

great Cham
emperor of the Mongols

embassage
errand

Harpy
birdlike monster with beautiful female face

In *Romeo and Juliet*, Juliet lists all the things she would rather do than marry Paris:

> O bid me leap, rather than marry Paris,
> From off the battlements of any tower,
> Or walk in thievish ways, or bid me lurk
> Where serpents are; chain me with roaring bears,
> Or hide me nightly in a charnel-house,
> O'ercovered quite with dead men's rattling bones,
> With reeky shanks and yellow chapless skulls;
> Or bid me go into a new-made grave,
> And hide me with a dead man in his shroud –

charnel-house
where bones and skulls were stored

reeky shanks
stinking legbones

chapless
without a jawbone

1. Both lists above are intensely physical. Act them out. As one person speaks the lines above very slowly, pausing after each item, the others perform the action.

2. Compile a list of all the things you would rather do than meet or marry someone not of your own choice. Try to follow the rhythms of Juliet's speech. Present a mimed version to the class to see if they can guess what you would rather do! Alternatively, your list might be about a quite different 'rather than ...'

Lists: a man, a city, a country

USE WITH PAGE 22

In *The Comedy of Errors*, descriptions pile up of Dr Pinch and the city of Ephesus:

anatomy
skeleton

mountebank
quack doctor

They brought one Pinch, a hungry, lean-faced villain,
A mere anatomy, a mountebank,
A threadbare juggler and a fortune teller,
A needy, hollow-eyed, sharp-looking wretch,
A living dead man.

cozenage
cheating

prating mountebanks
fast talking quack doctors

They say this town is full of cozenage,
As nimble jugglers that deceive the eye,
Dark-working sorcerers that change the mind,
Soul-killing witches that deform the body,
Disguisèd cheaters, prating mountebanks
And many suchlike liberties of sin.

In *King Richard II*, John of Gaunt paints a picture of England:

Mars
god of war

Eden
paradise, garden of delights

office
function

This royal throne of kings, this sceptred isle,
This earth of majesty, this seat of Mars,
This other Eden, demi-paradise,
This fortress built by Nature for herself
Against infection and the hand of war,
This happy breed of men, this little world,
This precious stone set in the silver sea
Which serves it in the office of a wall
Or as a moat defensive to a house
Against the envy of less happier lands,
This blessèd plot, this earth, this realm, this England

Speak aloud all the descriptions above. Select one as a model to compile your own description of either a person, a place or a country.

Lists: muddling them up

USE WITH PAGE 22

Shakespeare mocks the compiling of lists through Dogberry, the foolish constable in *Much Ado About Nothing*, who lists his complaints against the men he has arrested. Don Pedro replies mockingly in the same fashion.

belied
told lies about

DON PEDRO Officers, what offence have these men done?
DOGBERRY Marry, sir, they have committed false report, moreover they have spoken untruths, secondarily, they are slanders, sixth and lastly, they have belied a lady, thirdly they have verified unjust things, and to conclude, they are lying knaves.
DON PEDRO First I ask thee what they have done, thirdly I ask what's their offence, sixth and lastly why they are committed, and to conclude, what you lay to their charge?

1 Take parts and speak the lines in different ways. What can you deduce about Dogberry from his language?

2 Use Dogberry's list as the start of an improvisation in which he gives evidence against the men he has arrested.

3 Write a paragraph in Dogberry's style on 'Why I like (or dislike) Shakespeare'.

Alternatively, make up a list on a topic of your own choice.

Lists: rumours and gossip

USE WITH PAGE 22

In *King John*, Hubert tells how rumours are circulating about the death of Arthur and an invading French army.

beldams
old women

measure
tailor's ruler

contrary
wrong

embattailèd
in position for battle

artificer
workman

HUBERT My lord, they say five moons were seen tonight:
Four fixèd, and the fifth did whirl about
The other four in wondrous motion.
KING JOHN Five moons?
HUBERT Old men and beldams in the streets
Do prophesy upon it dangerously.
Young Arthur's death is common in their mouths,
And when they talk of him, they shake their heads,
And whisper one another in the ear.
And he that speaks doth gripe the hearer's wrist,
Whilst he that hears makes fearful action
With wrinkled brows, with nods, with rolling eyes.
I saw a smith stand with his hammer, thus,
The whilst his iron did on the anvil cool,
With open mouth swallowing a tailor's news,
Who, with his shears and measure in his hand,
Standing on slippers, which his nimble haste
Had falsely thrust upon contrary feet,
Told of a many thousand warlike French
That were embattailèd and ranked in Kent.
Another lean, unwashed artificer
Cuts off his tale and talks of Arthur's death.

1 Act out the description. Work in groups, and as one person slowly speaks the lines, the others act out everything described. How many different items can you find in Hubert's list?

2 Write a dozen or more lines of your own to describe how a rumour can spread like wildfire around your school or college. Use Hubert's lines as a model for your parody.

Verse

USE WITH ONE OF PAGES 29 to 35

Today, audiences expect films and television plays to use language which is everyday and familiar. But in Shakespeare's time, audiences expected actors, especially in histories and tragedies, to speak in verse. The 'poetic' style of verse was felt to be particularly suitable for kings, great affairs of war and state, or tragic themes.

Shakespeare's verse is written in iambic pentameter (which simply means that each line has five stresses). Typically the five stressed (/) syllables alternate with five unstressed (x) syllables, giving a ten-syllable line. To help you feel the rhythm, tap out the stresses:

x / x / x / x / x /
But soft, what light through yonder window breaks?

The danger when verse is analysed in this way is that it looks like algebra, and seems to suggest a mechanical, repetitive rhythm:

de *dum*, de *dum*, de *dum*, de *dum*, de *dum*

Actors always try to ensure that verse, rhymed or unrhymed (blank verse) does not sound boring and monotonous on stage. They use the clues that Shakespeare provides to match the rhythm to the thoughts and feelings of the characters.

In Shakespeare's early plays the rhythm of the verse tends to be very regular. The lines are often 'end-stopped', each line making sense on its own, with a pause at the end of the line. In *Titus Andronicus* (a very early play) Titus speaks in measured, formal style, even at the most melodramatic moments, as for example when he threatens the two men he intends to kill and bake in a pie:

coffin
pie crust

pasties
meat pies

Hark, villains, I will grind your bones to dust,
And with your blood and it I'll make a paste,
And of the paste a coffin I will rear,
And make two pasties of your shameful heads.

As Shakespeare's playwriting developed, he used fewer end-stopped lines. He made much greater use of enjambement (running on), where one line flows on into the next, seemingly without pause. *Macbeth*, for example, contains a great deal of enjambement:

sere
withered

I have lived long enough. My way of life
Is fall'n into the sere, the yellow leaf.

1 To experience the five-beat rhythm of iambic pentameter, speak Titus's lines aloud, and physically emphasise the five stresses: clap hands, tap your desk, or with a partner work out a rhythmical movement to accompany the lines. Do the same with the verse lines on the accompanying worksheet.

2 Feel the rhythm! Listen to your heartbeat and you can hear the basic rhythm of weak and strong stresses: de-*dum*, de-*dum*, de-*dum*.

3 Make up eight to ten lines of your own in iambic pentameter.

Verse: the death of Ophelia

USE WITH PAGE 28

In *Hamlet*, Gertrude reports how Ophelia drowned.

There is a willow grows askant a brook,
That shows his hoar leaves in the glassy stream.
Therewith fantastic garlands did she make,
Of crow-flowers, nettles, daisies, and long purples,
That liberal shepherds give a grosser name,
But our cold maids do dead men's fingers call them.
There on the pendant boughs her cronet weeds
Clamb'ring to hang, an envious sliver broke,
When down her weedy trophies and herself
Fell in the weeping brook. Her clothes spread wide,
And mermaid-like awhile they bore her up,
Which time she chanted snatches of old lauds
As one incapable of her own distress,
Or like a creature native and indued
Unto that element. But long it could not be
Till that her garments, heavy with their drink,
Pulled the poor wretch from her melodious lay
To muddy death.

askant
leaning over

hoar
grey

liberal
free-speaking

pendant
hanging

cronet
coronet, garland

sliver
branch

lauds
hymns

incapable of
uncomprehending

indued
adapted

lay
song

Ophelia, painting by John Everett Millais, 1852

How do you feel the lines should be spoken on stage? Imagine that the actress playing Gertrude asks, 'Should I speak them as poetry? Can you give me some advice, almost line by line, on how to deliver the speech?' Make your reply.

Verse: Othello's word music

USE WITH PAGE 28

Othello's style of speech is almost operatic, and his language has often been described as 'the Othello music'. Here, Othello, believing Desdemona to be unfaithful, prepares to kill her:

flaming minister
burning torch

Promethean heat
in Greek mythology, Prometheus stole fire from the gods to give life to mortals

relume
light again

Enter OTHELLO, *with a light, and* DESDEMONA *in bed*

OTHELLO It is the cause, it is the cause, my soul:
Let me not name it to you, you chaste stars.
It is the cause. Yet I'll not shed her blood,
Nor scar that whiter skin of hers than snow
And smooth as monumental alabaster –
Yet she must die, else she'll betray more men.
Put out the light, and then put out the light:
If I quench thee, thou flaming minister,
I can again thy former light restore,
Should I repent me; but once put out thy light,
Thou cunning'st pattern of excelling nature,
I know not where is that Promethean heat
That can thy light relume. When I have plucked thy rose,
I cannot give it vital growth again;
It needs must wither. I'll smell it on the tree.

He kisses her.

O balmy breath, that dost almost persuade
Justice to break her sword! One more, one more!
Be thus when thou art dead, and I will kill thee
And love thee after. One more, and this the last.
So sweet was ne'er so fatal. I must weep.
But they are cruel tears: this sorrow's heavenly –
It strikes where it doth love. She wakes.

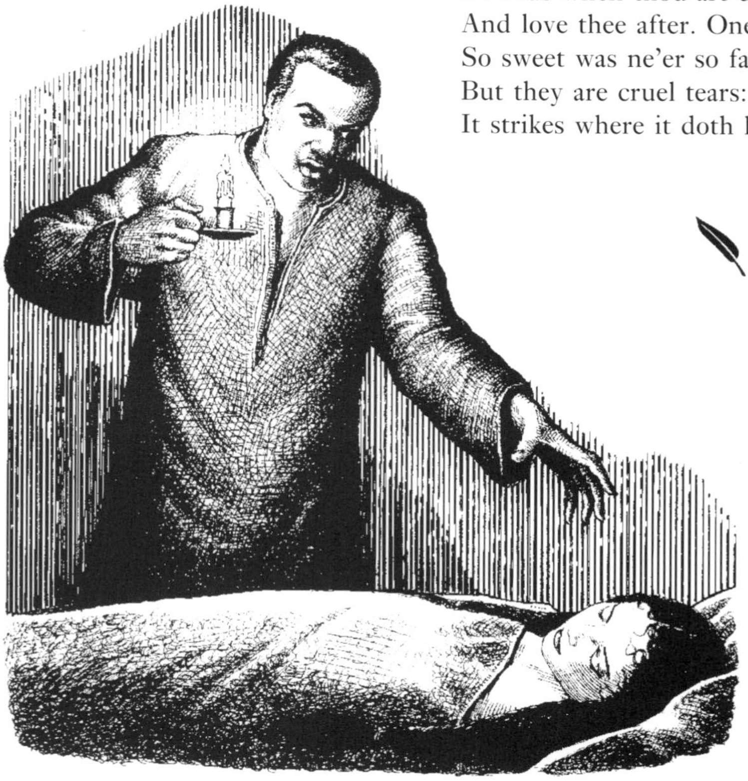

1 First, speak the lines very regularly, with five strong stresses in each line, and a marked pause at the end of each line. Then explore more effective ways to bring out Othello's thoughts and feelings.

2 Shakespeare often shapes a line into two sections divided by a pause (a caesura): 'Put out the light (*pause*), and then put out the light'. But he gives actors many other indications of where they might pause. Work through Othello's speech a line at a time, suggesting where he could pause and what actions he might perform.

Verse: too regular to be sincere?

USE WITH PAGE 28

King Richard II resigns himself to giving up his crown.

A God's name
in the name of God

set of beads
a rosary

gay apparel
fine clothes

almsman
man who receives charity

palmer
a pilgrim who has visited the Holy Land

trade
traffic

What must the king do now? Must he submit?
The king shall do it. Must he be deposed?
The king shall be contented. Must he lose
The name of king? A God's name let it go.
I'll give my jewels for a set of beads,
My gorgeous palace for a hermitage,
My gay apparel for an almsman's gown,
My figured goblets for a dish of wood,
My sceptre for a palmer's walking staff,
My subjects for a pair of carvèd saints,
And my large kingdom for a little grave,
A little, little grave, an obscure grave.
Or I'll be buried in the king's highway,
Some way of common trade, where subjects' feet
May hourly trample on their sovereign's head;
For on my heart they tread now whilst I live,
And buried once, why not upon my head?

1. In one stage production, Richard spoke the lines as a panicky gabble, very 'unpoetically'. In another he spoke them as a solemn religious ritual. And in another, he emphasised the antitheses (jewels/beads, etc.) by turning first one way then another. Experiment with different ways of speaking to find a version you prefer.

2. Some people say that because of the regularity of the verse, Richard is evidently not sincere. Give reasons for your agreement or disagreement with that view. To help you decide, speak the lines in a way that emphasises the five-beat rhythm of each line.

Verse: Hermia and Helena

USE WITH PAGE 28

In *A Midsummer Night's Dream*, Helena asks Hermia for advice about how to attract Demetrius.

lodestars
guiding stars

favour
personal qualities (appearance, voice etc.)

bated
excepted

HERMIA God speed, fair Helena! Whither away?
HELENA Call you me fair? That 'fair' again unsay.
Demetrius loves your fair: O happy fair!
Your eyes are lodestars, and your tongue's sweet air
More tuneable than lark to shepherd's ear
When wheat is green, when hawthorn buds appear.
Sickness is catching. O, were favour so,
Yours would I catch, fair Hermia, ere I go;
My ear should catch your voice, my eye your eye,
My tongue should catch your tongue's sweet melody.
Were the world mine, Demetrius being bated,
The rest I'd give to be to you translated.
O, teach me how you look, and with what art
You sway the motion of Demetrius' heart.
HERMIA I frown upon him; yet he loves me still.
HELENA O that your frowns would teach my smiles such skill!
HERMIA I give him curses; yet he gives me love.
HELENA O that my prayers could such affection move!
HERMIA The more I hate, the more he follows me.
HELENA The more I love, the more he hateth me.
HERMIA His folly, Helena, is no fault of mine.
HELENA None but your beauty; would that fault were mine!
HERMIA Take comfort: he no more shall see my face;
Lysander and myself will fly this place.

1 The verse is very strongly patterned, written in rhyming couplets. Take parts and speak the lines, first emphasising very formally the rhymes and repetitions. Second, try to speak them as a modern 'unpoetic' conversation. Find what you think is an appropriate style of speaking.

2 Experiment with physical ways in which you can emphasise the very regular rhythm of the lines: for example, walking five paces to accompany each line, tapping out five beats on your desk, or working out a movement with a partner and so on.

3 Invent eight additional lines for Helena and Hermia in the same style and on the same topic.

Verse: shared lines

USE WITH PAGE 28

A line can be 'loosened' by dividing it between one or more characters. There are many such lines in *Antony and Cleopatra* in which Shakespeare frequently runs on meaning and rhythm from one line to the next, often sharing lines between two speakers. In this example, Cleopatra and Eros help Antony put on his armour:

ANTONY If fortune be not ours today, it is
Because we brave her. Come.
CLEOPATRA Nay I'll help too.
What's this for?
ANTONY Ah, let be, let be! Thou art
The armourer of my heart. False, false; this, this.
CLEOPATRA Sooth, la, I'll help. Thus it must be.
ANTONY Well, Well,
We shall thrive now. Seest thou, my good fellow?
Go, put on thy defences.
EROS Briefly, sir
CLEOPATRA Is not this buckled well?
ANTONY Rarely, rarely.

It is a stage convention that shared lines are spoken with little or no pause between speakers. According to this custom, the half line acts as a cue for the other actor, rather than a pause. In this single line from *King John*, John orders Hubert to murder Arthur.

JOHN Death.
HUBERT My Lord?
JOHN A grave.
HUBERT He shall not live.
JOHN Enough.

1. Is it always dramatically effective to obey the stage convention on shared lines (that there is no pause between speakers)? Take parts and experiment with the lines above from *Antony and Cleopatra*. Try it also with the single line from *King John*. Speak the lines in a number of different ways, without and with pauses.
2. Identify some shared lines in the play you are studying. Decide how you think they might be spoken on stage.
3. Try your hand at writing some shared lines. Select two Shakespeare characters and invent a dialogue between them.

Verse: find the lines 1

USE WITH PAGE 28

In the following extracts, Shakespeare's blank verse has been printed as prose, with all punctuation removed and with no capital letters.

A but soft what light through yonder window breaks it is the east and juliet is the sun arise fair sun and kill the envious moon who is already sick and pale with grief that thou her maid art far more fair than she

B two households both alike in dignity in fair verona where we lay our scene from ancient grudge break to new mutiny where civil blood makes civil hands unclean from forth the fatal loins of these two foes a pair of star crossed lovers take their life whose misadventured piteous overthrows doth with their death bury their parents strife the fearful passage of their death marked love and the continuance of their parents rage which but their childrens end naught could remove is now the two hours traffic of our stage the which if you with patient ears attend what here shall miss our toil shall strive to mend

C if music be the food of love play on give me excess of it that surfeiting the appetite may sicken and so die that strain again it had a dying fall o it came oer my ear like the sweet sound that breathes upon a bank of violets stealing and giving odour enough no more tis not so sweet now as it was before o spirit of love how quick and fresh art thou that notwithstanding thy capacity receiveth as the sea naught enters there of what validity and pitch soeer but falls into abatement and low price even in a minute so full of shapes is fancy that it alone is high fantastical

---

Turn the passages back into verse lines. Remember, there are usually five stressed syllables in each line (iambic pentameter), but because Shakespeare used verse so flexibly, it is best to speak the words aloud, trying to find the rhythm. For example, extract B should start like this:

> *Two households, both alike in dignity,*
> *In fair Verona, where we lay our scene,*
> *From ancient grudge …*

Verse: find the lines 2

USE WITH PAGE 28

In the following extracts, Shakespeare's blank verse has been printed as prose, with all punctuation removed and with no capital letters.

D how if when i am laid into the tomb i wake before the time that romeo come to redeem me theres a fearful point shall i not then be stifled in the vault to whose foul mouth no healthsome air breathes in and there die strangled ere my romeo comes or if i live is it not very like the horrible conceit of death and night together with the terror of the place as in a vault an ancient receptacle where for this many hundred years the bones of all my buried ancestors are packed where bloody tybalt yet but green in earth lies festering in his shroud where as they say at some hours in the night spirits resort alack alack is it not like that i so early waking what with loathsome smells and shrieks like mandrakes torn out of the earth that living mortals hearing them run mad

E rebellious subjects enemies to peace profaners of this neighbour stained steel will they not hear what ho you men you beasts that quench the fire of your pernicious rage with purple fountains issuing from your veins on pain of torture from those bloody hands throw your mistempered weapons to the ground and hear the sentence of your moved prince

F three civil brawls bred of an airy word by thee old capulet and montague have thrice disturbed the quiet of our streets and made veronas ancient citizens cast by their grave beseeming ornaments to wield old partisans in hands as old cankered with peace to part your cankered hate if ever you disturb our streets again your lives shall pay the forfeit of the peace for this time all the rest depart away you capulet shall go along with me and montague come you this afternoon to know our farther pleasure in this case to old free town our common judgement place once more on pain of death all men depart

G where shall we dine o me what fray was here yet tell me not for i have heard it all heres much to do with hate but more with love why then o brawling love o loving hate o any thing of nothing first create o heavy lightness serious vanity misshapen chaos of well seeming forms feather of lead bright smoke cold fire sick health still waking sleep that is not what it is this love feel i that feel no love in this

---

Turn the passages back into verse lines. Remember, there are usually five stressed syllables in each line (iambic pentameter), but because Shakespeare used verse so flexibly, it is best to speak the words aloud, trying to find the rhythm.

Verse: tetrameter 1

USE WITH PAGE 37

When a verse line has four stresses, its rhythm is called tetrameter (Greek tetra = four).

Round about the cauldron go;
In the poisoned entrails throw.

Tetrameter is the common rhythm of nursery rhymes (for example, 'Jack and Jill went up the hill'). Shakespeare uses it for songs, the witches' chants in *Macbeth*, doggerel poetry (for example, Orlando's verses in *As You Like It*), and the Duke's soliloquy in *Measure for Measure*. In *A Midsummer Night's Dream*, Puck and the fairies often speak in tetrameter rhythm.

Only one of Shakespeare's sonnets (number 145) is written in tetrameter. Some scholars think that it was written by Shakespeare in his youth to his future wife Anne Hathaway. They suggest that in line 13 'hate away' might be a pun on Hathaway, and that line 14 could be spoken as 'Anne saved my life'.

Love's
Venus' or Cupid's

languished
pined, suffered depression

Straight
immediately

Chiding
scolding, rebuking

gentle doom
kind judgement

Those lips that Love's own hand did make
Breathed forth the sound that said 'I hate'
To me that languished for her sake;
But when she saw my woeful state,
Straight in her heart did mercy come,
Chiding that tongue that ever sweet
Was used in giving gentle doom,
And taught it thus anew to greet:
'I hate' she altered with an end
That followed it as gentle day
Doth follow night, who like a fiend
From heaven to hell is flown away:
'I hate' from hate away she threw,
And saved my life, saying 'not you'.

---

1 Speak Sonnet 145 aloud, emphasising the four stresses in each line. Then step into role as the young William Shakespeare and write your own sonnet to Anne Hathaway, using Sonnet 145 as a model.

2 Close your eyes and think of any poems or verse that come into your mind. Are they in tetrameter ('four beat' rhythm)? Make a list of any poems or verses you remember and identify how many of them are in tetrameter rhythm.

Verse: tetrameter 2

USE WITH PAGE 36

In *A Midsummer Night's Dream*, Puck and the fairies often speak in tetrameter rhythm.

PUCK Now the hungry lion roars,
And the wolf behowls the moon,
Whilst the heavy ploughman snores,
All with weary task foredone.
Now the wasted brands do glow,
Whilst the screech-owl, screeching loud,
Puts the wretch that lies in woe
In remembrance of a shroud.
Now it is the time of night
That the graves, all gaping wide,
Every one lets forth his sprite
In the church-way paths to glide.
And we fairies, that do run
By the triple Hecate's team
From the presence of the sun,
Following darkness like a dream,
Now are frolic; not a mouse
Shall disturb this hallowed house.
I am sent with broom before
To sweep the dust behind the door.

❖ ❖ ❖ ❖

FAIRY Over hill, over dale,
Thorough bush, thorough briar,
Over park, over pale,
Thorough flood, thorough fire;
I do wander everywhere
Swifter than the moon's sphere;
And I serve the Fairy Queen,
To dew her orbs upon the green.
The cowslips tall her pensioners be;
In their gold coats spots you see –
Those be rubies, fairy favours,
In those freckles live their savours.
I must go seek some dewdrops here,
And hang a pearl in every cowslip's ear.

1 Puck's lines conjure up a night world in which he and his fellow spirits are free to play. Work in a group and prepare an active way of presenting his lines to greatest dramatic effect.

2 A spirit tells how she travels everywhere to serve Titania, her queen. Work out a staging of the lines.

Rhyme

USE WITH PAGE 39

Rhyme in verse involves matching sounds at the ends of each line. It gives an audible pattern to language and makes speech easier to learn:

> When shall we three meet again?
> In thunder, lightning, or in rain?

Shakespeare uses rhyme in songs, prologues and epilogues, masques and plays within plays, and for the supernatural, for example the witches in *Macbeth* or the fairies in *A Midsummer Night's Dream*.

Long speeches in blank verse (unrhymed) often end with a rhyming couplet. So too do many scenes or acts. The Elizabethan stage did not have the sophisticated technology (lights, curtains) to signal the end of a scene. So Shakespeare often provides his characters with a strong rhyming couplet to accompany their exit, and as a cue for other actors to enter. As Macbeth leaves to murder Duncan he hears the bell:

> Hear it not, Duncan, for it is a knell
> That summons thee to heaven or to hell.

In *Love's Labour's Lost* Biron rhymingly laughs at people who are too serious about learning from books. His three friends try to mock him, but he wins the exchange with a rhyme on rhyme:

deep-searched well understood

continual plodders unthinking readers

earthly godfathers scholars

wot know

proceeded argued

proceeding understanding

green geese are a-breeding young geese are cackling

BIRON Study is like the heaven's glorious sun,
That will not be deep-search'd with saucy looks;
Small have continual plodders ever won,
Save base authority from others' books.
These earthly godfathers of heaven's lights,
That give a name to every fixèd star,
Have no more profit of their shining nights
Than those that walk and wot not what they are.
Too much to know is to know nought but fame;
And every godfather can give a name.
KING How well he's read, to reason against reading!
DUMAINE Proceeded well, to stop all good proceeding!
LONGAVILLE He weeds the corn, and still lets grow the weeding.
BIRON The spring is near, when green geese are a-breeding.
DUMAINE How follows that?
BIRON Fit in his place and time.
DUMAINE In reason nothing.
BIRON Something then in rhyme.

1 In groups of four, take parts and speak the lines above to emphasise the rhymes. How might such rhymed lines be performed on stage?

2 Search through the play you are currently studying for examples of use of rhyme. Look particularly at scene endings.

Rhyme: Shakespeare mocks rhymers

USE WITH PAGE 38

In *Much Ado About Nothing* Benedick regrets his inability to find rhymes:

> I can find out no rhyme to lady but baby, an innocent rhyme: for scorn horn, a hard rhyme: for school fool, a babbling rhyme: very ominous endings. No, I was not born under a rhyming planet ...

In A *Midsummer Night's Dream*, the mechanicals stage a play. Thisbe (played by Flute) laments over the dead body of Pyramus (played by Bottom).

sisters three
goddesses of fate

gore
blood

shore
cut

imbrue
stab, make bloody

Asleep, my love?
What, dead, my dove?
O Pyramus, arise.
Speak, speak! Quite dumb?
Dead, dead? A tomb
Must cover thy sweet eyes.
These lily lips,
This cherry nose,
These yellow cowslip cheeks
Are gone, are gone.
Lovers, make moan;
His eyes were green as leeks.
O sisters three,
Come, come to me
With hands as pale as milk;
Lay them in gore,
Since you have shore
With shears his thread of silk.
Tongue, not a word!
Come, trusty sword,
Come blade, my breast imbrue! *[Stabs herself.]*
And farewell, friends.
Thus Thisbe ends –
Adieu, adieu, adieu! *[Dies.]*

1 Step into role as Thisbe and be a star!

2 Shakespeare mocks many of the conventions of poetry in Thisbe's speech. Try your hand at writing a similar speech to 'send up' a well known Shakespeare play (for example, Juliet lamenting over Romeo).

Prose

USE WITH ONE OF PAGES 41 to 45

How did Shakespeare decide whether his characters should speak in verse or prose? A rough answer is that he followed the stage conventions of his time. It was conventional for prose to be used:

- in proclamations, written challenges or accusations, and letters, for example, Macbeth's letter to Lady Macbeth telling of his meeting with the witches.
- by low status characters: servants, clowns, drunks. The low status villains, Iago in *Othello* and Edmund in *King Lear*, speak many prose lines.
- to express madness: King Lear, Hamlet, Edgar as Poor Tom, and Lady Macbeth (all high status) express their madness, or assumed madness, in prose.
- for comedy: Falstaff and Sir Toby Belch, both knights (high status), use prose as comic characters. Among Shakespeare's comedies, almost ninety per cent of *The Merry Wives of Windsor* is prose, and over half of *Twelfth Night*, *As You Like It* and *Much Ado About Nothing*.

But Shakespeare never followed any rule slavishly, and you can always finds exceptions to the conventions. Low status characters, for example, Juliet's Nurse and Caliban, sometimes speak verse, and high status characters switch to prose, for example, King Henry V. After the assassination of Julius Caesar, Brutus uses prose for his speech to the citizens of Rome, but Antony uses verse.

The context of a speech sometimes explains why prose or verse is spoken. For example, Macbeth speaks some prose when talking to the low status murderers. The villainous Iago typically speaks prose, but switches to verse when he is with Othello.

1 Check through the play you are currently studying to discover who uses verse and who uses prose. Suggest reasons for the difference.

2 As you work on the prose lines on the accompanying worksheet, look out for imagery, lists and patterns (repeated words and phrases, balanced contrasts). They will help your understanding of character, mood and tone.

3 Write a set of 'director's notes': advice to the actors on how the speech might be performed in a dramatically effective way. For example, are there pauses? Should repeated words be stressed? What pace, tone and volume should the actors use? Then speak and act out the language!

Prose: look for a pattern

USE WITH PAGE 40

In *The Comedy of Errors*, Dromio of Ephesus complains about his treatment by his master:

wont her brat
usually bears (or beats) her child

When I am cold, he heats me with beating; when I am warm, he cools me with beating; I am waked with it when I sleep, raised with it when I sit, driven out of doors with it when I go from home, welcomed home with it when I return; nay, I bear it on my shoulders, as a beggar wont her brat, and I think when he hath lamed me I shall beg with it from door to door.

Prose is not so obviously patterned as verse, but Shakespeare's prose often has strong symmetry, particularly in the plays he wrote early in his career. Dromio's prose can be set out to show its structures and rhythms:

When I am cold	he heats me with beating
When I am warm	he cools me with beating;
I am waked with it	when I sleep
raised with it	when I sit
driven out of doors with it	when I go from home
welcomed home with it	when I return
nay I bear it on my shoulders	as a beggar wont her brat
And I think	when he hath lamed me
I shall beg with it	from door to door

Macbeth's Porter describes the effects of drink:

lechery
lust

equivocator
someone who juggles with the truth

giving him the lie
tricking him

Lechery, sir, it provokes, and unprovokes: it provokes the desire, but it takes away the performance. Therefore much drink may be said to be an equivocator with lechery: it makes him, and it mars him; it sets him on, and it takes him off; it persuades him and disheartens him, makes him stand to and not stand to. In conclusion, equivocates him in a sleep, and giving him the lie, leaves him.

Use the method of setting out prose to reveal the pattern of balanced contrasts used by Porter in the extract above.

Prose: falling in love

USE WITH PAGE 40

In *Much Ado About Nothing*, Benedick reflects on how love has changed his friend and fellow-soldier Claudio. Might he too fall in love? Very unlikely! He goes on to list the virtues required of his own future wife.

argument
object

drum and the fife
music of war

tabor and the pipe
music of peace

carving
designing

wont
accustomed

turned orthography
speaking flowery language

oyster
i.e. shut up in moody silence

noble/angel
names of coins

I do much wonder, that one man seeing how much another man is a fool, when he dedicates his behaviours to love, will after he hath laughed at such shallow follies in others, become the argument of his own scorn, by falling in love: and such a man is Claudio. I have known when there was no music with him but the drum and the fife, and now had he rather hear the tabor and the pipe: I have known when he would have walked ten mile afoot, to see a good armour, and now will he lie ten nights awake carving the fashion of a new doublet: he was wont to speak plain and to the purpose (like an honest man and a soldier) and now is he turned orthography, his words are a very fantastical banquet, just so many strange dishes: may I be so converted and see with these eyes? I cannot tell, I think not: I will not be sworn but love may transform me to an oyster, but I'll take my oath on it, till he have made an oyster of me, he shall never make me such a fool: one woman is fair, yet I am well: another is wise, yet I am well: another virtuous, yet I am well: but till all graces be in one woman, one woman shall not come in my grace: rich she shall be, that's certain: wise, or I'll none: virtuous, or I'll never cheapen her: fair, or I'll never look on her: mild, or come not near me: noble, or not I for an angel: of good discourse, an excellent musician – and her hair shall be of what colour it please God.

Benedick's prose is strongly patterned. Work out a presentation with accompanying actions to show what Benedick describes.

Prose: advice to actors

USE WITH PAGE 40

Hamlet instructs the Players on acting style.

trippingly
lightly

as lief
rather

robustious
violent, loud-mouthed

periwig-pated
wig-wearing

groundlings
poorest theatre-goers who stood in the open yard in front of the stage

capable of
understand

Termagant/Herod
noisy, raging characters in medieval Mystery plays

modesty
moderation

Speak the speech I pray you as I pronounced it to you, trippingly on the tongue; but if you mouth it as many of our players do, I had as lief the town-crier spoke my lines. Nor do not saw the air too much with your hand thus, but use all gently; for in the very torrent, tempest, and, as I may say, whirlwind of your passion, you must acquire and beget a temperance that may give it smoothness. Oh, it offends me to the soul to hear a robustious periwig-pated fellow tear a passion to totters, to very rags, to split the ears of the groundlings, who for the most part are capable of nothing but inexplicable dumb-shows and noise. I would have such a fellow whipped for o'erdoing Termagant – it out-Herods Herod. Pray you avoid it.

Be not too tame neither, but let your own discretion be your tutor. Suit the action to the word, the word to the action, with this special observance, that you o'erstep not the modesty of nature. For anything so o'erdone is from the purpose of playing, whose end both at the first and now, was and is, to hold as 'twere the mirror up to nature; to show virtue her own feature, scorn her own image, and the very age and body of the time his form and pressure ...

... And let those that play your clowns speak no more than is set down for them, for there be of them that will themselves laugh, to set on some quantity of barren spectators to laugh too, though in the meantime some necessary question of the play be then to be considered. That's villainous, and shows a most pitiful ambition in the fool that uses it.

Follow Hamlet's advice and speak his lines with appropriate actions.

Prose: melancholy – and man

USE WITH PAGE 40

Hamlet tells of the effect that his melancholy has on him. He has lost delight in the splendours of the earth, heavens and humankind itself.

firmament
heavens, sky

express
well-made

apprehension
understanding

paragon
ideal of excellence

I have of late, but wherefore I know not, lost all my mirth, forgone all custom of exercises; and indeed it goes so heavily with my disposition that this goodly frame, the earth, seems to me a sterile promontory; this most excellent canopy the air, look you, this brave o'erhanging firmament, this majestical roof fretted with golden fire – why, it appeareth no other thing to me but a foul and pestilent congregation of vapours. What a piece of work is a man! How noble in reason, how infinite in faculties, in form and moving how express and admirable, in action how like an angel, in apprehension how like a god! The beauty of the world, the paragon of animals – and yet to me, what is this quintessence of dust? Man delights not me – no, nor woman neither, though by your smiling you seem to say so.

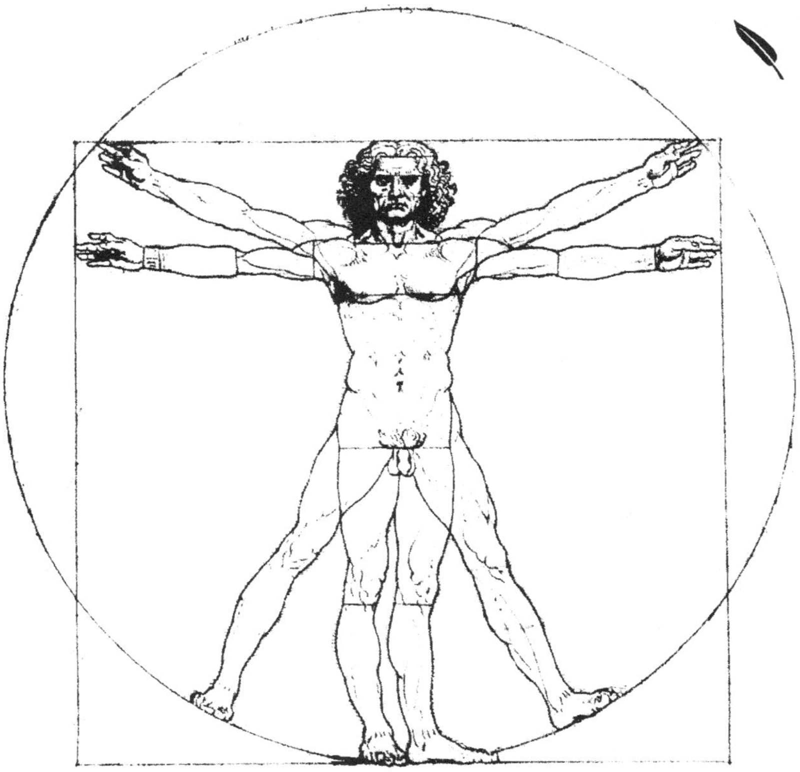

'What a piece of work is a man!'
Drawing by Leonardo da Vinci, 1490

1. What is Hamlet's tone: disillusioned, sincere, sarcastic, bitter, awestruck, seemingly demented? Or does his mood vary in different parts of his speech? Rehearse and deliver your own performance of the lines.
2. This example of Hamlet's prose has often been claimed to have the qualities of poetry. Write out the lines as verse and speak your 'poetic' version. Make a list of what you think are the differences between treating the lines as dramatic speech, and treating them as poetry.

Prose: expressing madness

USE WITH PAGE 40

In *King Lear*, Edgar, pretending to be a madman (Poor Tom), speaks prose.

halters in his pew
hangman's nooses in his seat in church

ratsbane
poison

course
hunt

star-blasting and taking
catching infectious diseases caused by stars (a belief of astrology)

Who gives anything to Poor Tom, whom the foul fiend hath led through fire and through flame, through ford and whirlpool, o'er bog and quagmire; that hath laid knives under his pillow and halters in his pew; set ratsbane by his porridge; made him proud of heart to ride on a bay trotting-horse over four-inched bridges, to course his own shadow for a traitor. Bless thy five wits, Tom's a-cold! O do, de, do, de, do de. Bless thee from whirlwinds, star-blasting, and taking. Do Poor Tom some charity, whom the foul fiend vexes. There could I have him now, and there, and there again, and there.

'Poor Tom, that eats the swimming frog, the toad, the tadpole, the wall-newt, and the water ...'

The stage convention of Shakespeare's time was that mad characters spoke prose, not verse. Speak and act out Edgar's lines, then invent some more 'mad' language for him in the same style.

Rhetoric: the art of persuasion

USE WITH ONE OF PAGES 47 to 51

Today, the word 'rhetoric' is used to describe language that is insincere and artificial, not to be trusted. But in Shakespeare's time, rhetoric enjoyed high status and was taught in schools. As a schoolboy, Shakespeare would have learned by heart well over one hundred 'figures' of rhetoric, and he used most of them in his plays.

For Shakespeare and his contemporaries, rhetoric was the art of persuasion. It involved all the ways of using language that make it more persuasive, gaining the confidence of listeners, and appealing to their reason, their emotions and their imagination.

In this example, Macbeth tries to persuade the suspicious Macduff that he simply could not stop himself from killing the two bodyguards of the murdered Duncan:

temp'rate even-tempered
Th'expedition the haste
the pauser, reason delaying thought
Unmannerly breached rudely covered
gore blood
make's make his

MACBETH O, yet I do repent me of my fury
That I did kill them.
MACDUFF Wherefore did you so?
MACBETH Who can be wise, amazed, temp'rate, and furious,
Loyal and neutral, in a moment? No man.
Th'expedition of my violent love
Outran the pauser, reason. Here lay Duncan,
His silver skin laced with his golden blood
And his gashed stabs looked like a breach in nature,
For ruin's wasteful entrance. There the murderers,
Steeped in the colours of their trade; their daggers
Unmannerly breeched with gore. Who could refrain,
That had a heart to love and in that heart
Courage to make's love known?

Take parts as Macduff and Macbeth. Speak the lines several times in different ways: sincerely, in panic, angrily, etc. Then talk together about what Macbeth says:

a Is it a logical argument?

b How does it appeal to the emotions and the imagination? Think about his use of imagery, all kinds of repetitions, lists, etc.

c Does it give the speaker an air of authority, and gain the confidence of the listeners?

d Is it effective? Will the speech achieve the speaker's intentions, and persuade the listeners?

e How should the speech be spoken to be most persuasive?

Rhetoric: persuading soldiers

USE WITH PAGE 46

Henry V urges his soldiers to attack Harfleur once again.

Once more unto the breach, dear friends, once more,
Or close the wall up with our English dead!
In peace there's nothing so becomes a man
As modest stillness and humility.
But when the blast of war blows in our ears,
Then imitate the action of the tiger:
Stiffen the sinews, conjure up the blood,
Disguise fair nature with hard-favoured rage.
Then lend the eye a terrible aspect,
Let it pry through the portage of the head,
Like the brass cannon. Let the brow o'erwhelm it
As fearfully as doth a gallèd rock
O'erhang and jutty his confounded base,
Swilled with the wild and wasteful ocean.
Now set the teeth and stretch the nostril wide,
Hold hard the breath, and bend up every spirit
To his full height. On, on, you noble English,
Whose blood is fet from fathers of war-proof,
Fathers that like so many Alexanders
Have in these parts from morn till even fought,
And sheathed their swords for lack of argument.
Dishonour not your mothers. Now attest
That those whom you called fathers did beget you.
Be copy now to men of grosser blood,
And teach them how to war.
And you, good yeomen,
Whose limbs were made in England, show us here
The mettle of your pasture. Let us swear
That you are worth your breeding, which I doubt not,
For there is none of you so mean and base
That hath not noble lustre in your eyes.
I see you stand like greyhounds in the slips,
Straining upon the start. The game's afoot.
Follow your spirit, and upon this charge
Cry 'God for Harry, England and Saint George!'

breach
gap in the defences

portage
portholes (eye sockets)

jutty ... base
jut out over its worn-away base

fet
derived, descended

Alexanders
Alexander the Great (supposedly the greatest soldier ever)

attest
give proof

grosser blood
lower social status

yeomen
ordinary soldiers

The mettle of your pasture
the fine stuff you are made of

in the slips
on their leads

---

1 Pick out all the ways in which Henry's language is intended to motivate his soldiers. Use questions a–e on page 46 to help you.

2 One actor compared the speech to driving a car; 'You start at the top, then you have to change down to first, up to second, to third, to fourth, to overdrive – and at the end still have trumpet and clarion left'. Divide up the lines in the light of this comment. Create sound effects for each section (snarling, stamping, clashings, etc.). Then rehearse and perform the speech.

Rhetoric: justifying a killing

USE WITH PAGE 46

Brutus tells the people of Rome why he assassinated Julius Caesar.

lovers
friends

bondman
slave

rude
uncivilised

question of his death is enrolled
reason for his assassination are recorded

enforced
exaggerated

Romans, countrymen, and lovers, hear me for my cause, and be silent that you may hear. Believe me for mine honour, and have respect to mine honour that you may believe. Censure me in your wisdom, and awake your senses that you may the better judge. If there be any in this assembly, any dear friend of Caesar's, to him I say that Brutus' love to Caesar was no less than his. If then that friend demand why Brutus rose against Caesar, this is my answer: not that I loved Caesar less, but that I loved Rome more. Had you rather Caesar were living, and die all slaves, than that Caesar were dead, to live all freemen? As Caesar loved me, I weep for him; as he was fortunate, I rejoice at it; as he was valiant, I honour him; but, as he was ambitious, I slew him. There is tears for his love, joy for his fortune, honour for his valour, and death for his ambition. Who is here so base that would be a bondman? If any, speak, for him have I offended. Who is here so rude that would not be a Roman? If any, speak, for him have I offended. Who is here so vile that will not love his country? If any, speak, for him have I offended. I pause for a reply.

ALL None, Brutus, none.

BRUTUS Then none have I offended. I have done no more to Caesar than you shall do to Brutus. The question of his death is enrolled in the Capitol, his glory not extenuated wherein he was worthy, nor his offences enforced for which he suffered death.

1 Brutus uses simple language, but his speech is carefully constructed to persuade the citizens of Rome and justify the assassination. Speak it several times, then identify the language devices that make it effective persuasion: repetitions, lists, antitheses, rhythm, etc.

2 Use questions a–e on page 46 to help you judge how persuasive you feel the speech to be.

Rhetoric: persuading citizens

USE WITH PAGE 46

Antony, political friend of the assassinated Julius Caesar, begins his speech to the citizens of Rome. He intends to turn them against Brutus and the other conspirators who killed Caesar.

interrèd
buried

general coffers
chests of money for the public good

Lupercal
day of festival

cause withholds
reason prevents

Friends, Romans, countrymen, lend me your ears!
I come to bury Caesar, not to praise him.
The evil that men do lives after them,
The good is oft interrèd with their bones:
So let it be with Caesar. The noble Brutus
Hath told you Caesar was ambitious;
If it were so, it was a grievous fault,
And grievously hath Caesar answered it.
Here, under leave of Brutus and the rest –
For Brutus is an honourable man,
So are they all, all honourable men –
Come I to speak in Caesar's funeral.
He was my friend, faithful and just to me,
But Brutus says he was ambitious,
And Brutus is an honourable man.
He hath brought many captives home to Rome,
Whose ransoms did the general coffers fill;
Did this in Caesar seem ambitious?
When that the poor have cried, Caesar hath wept:
Ambition should be made of sterner stuff;
Yet Brutus says he was ambitious,
And Brutus is an honourable man.
You all did see that on the Lupercal
I thrice presented him a kingly crown,
Which he did thrice refuse. Was this ambition?
Yet Brutus says he was ambitious,
And sure he is an honourable man.
I speak not to disprove what Brutus spoke,
But here I am to speak what I do know.
You all did love him once, not without cause;
What cause withholds you then to mourn for him?
O judgement, thou art fled to brutish beasts,
And men have lost their reason! Bear with me,
My heart is in the coffin there with Caesar,
And I must pause till it come back to me.

1 This is only the beginning of Antony's speech, but it displays all the powerful persuasive language devices he will use. Questions a–e on page 46 will help you identify the rhetorical devices he uses: repetition, rhythm, lists, antitheses, etc.

2 Practise speaking the lines, then work out and stage a performance.

USE WITH PAGE 46

Rhetoric: self-persuasion

trammel up the consequence
catch (like netting a fish) the result

surcease
death

jump the life to come
avoid Heaven's punishment

inventor
original teacher

chalice
cup, goblet

faculties
powers as a king

cherubin
angelic children

sightless couriers
wind (blind or invisible runners)

Macbeth struggles with his conscience. Should he kill King Duncan?

If it were done when 'tis done, then 'twere well
It were done quickly. If th'assassination
Could trammel up the consequence and catch
With his surcease, success, that but this blow
Might be the be-all and the end-all – here,
But here, upon this bank and shoal of time,
We'd jump the life to come. But in these cases,
We still have judgement here that we but teach
Bloody instructions, which being taught, return
To plague th'inventor. This even-handed justice
Commends th'ingredience of our poisoned chalice
To our own lips. He's here in double trust:
First, as I am his kinsman and his subject,
Strong both against the deed; then, as his host,
Who should against his murderer shut the door,
Not bear the knife myself. Besides, this Duncan
Hath borne his faculties so meek, hath been
So clear in his great office, that his virtues
Will plead like angels, trumpet-tongued against
The deep damnation of his taking-off.
And pity, like a naked newborn babe
Striding the blast, or heaven's cherubin horsed
Upon the sightless couriers of the air,
Shall blow the horrid deed in every eye,
That tears shall drown the wind. I have no spur
To prick the sides of my intent, but only
Vaulting ambition which o'erleaps itself
And falls on th'other –

1. Macbeth's soliloquy can be spoken like an anxious conversation between two people, who fearfully consider arguments against the murder. Work with a partner and share the speech between you in that way. Whispering adds extra tension!
2. Catch the see-sawing effect of Macbeth's thoughts, by joining hands and gently pushing or pulling as you speak, expressing the rhythms of each phrase, line or sentence.
3. Identify the reasons Macbeth gives to talk himself out of the murder. Suggest what he may have decided at the final line. Use questions a–e on page 46 to help you.
4. Stage the lines!

Rhetoric: kill the king!

USE WITH PAGE 46

Macbeth has had doubts about his previous desire to kill Duncan. Lady Macbeth persuades him to do the murder.

the ornament of life
life's highest achievement (the crown)

wait upon
delay, prevent

cat i'th'adage
cat in the proverb (who wanted to eat the fish, but feared the water)

break this enterprise
suggest killing Duncan

They have made themselves
now is the time and place to do the murder

fitness
timeliness

given suck
suckled a child at my breast

had I sworn
if I had promised

LADY MACBETH Was the hope drunk
Wherein you dressed yourself? Hath it slept since?
And wakes it now to look so green and pale
At what it did so freely? From this time,
Such I account thy love. Art thou afeard
To be the same in thine own act and valour,
As thou art in desire? Wouldst thou have that
Which thou esteem'st the ornament of life,
And live a coward in thine own esteem,
Letting I dare not wait upon I would,
Like the poor cat i'th'adage?
MACBETH Prithee, peace.
I dare do all that may become a man;
Who dares do more is none.
LADY MACBETH What beast was't then
That made you break this enterprise to me?
When you durst do it, then you were a man.
And to be more than what you were, you would
Be so much more the man. Nor time, nor place
Did then adhere, and yet you would make both.
They have made themselves and that their fitness now
Does unmake you. I have given suck and know
How tender 'tis to love the babe that milks me:
I would, while it was smiling in my face,
Have plucked my nipple from his boneless gums
And dashed the brains out, had I so sworn
As you have done to this.

1. Step into role and explore different ways of speaking the lines: whisper, hiss, threaten, wheedle, etc.
2. Identify the ways in which Lady Macbeth plays upon Macbeth's male self-esteem, and appeals to his courage, soldierliness, manhood and ambition. Which words and phrases do you think would have most force in persuading Macbeth? Use questions a–e on page 46 to help you.
3. Share Lady Macbeth's speech between group members and prepare a choral-speaking version.

Hyperbole 1

USE WITH PAGE 53

Hyperbole is extravagant and obvious exaggeration – as when someone today says 'I'm dying for a drink'. Prince Hal describes Falstaff as a 'huge hill of flesh'. Othello, tortured by the knowledge that he has wrongly killed Desdemona, exclaims:

Blow me about in winds! Roast me in sulphur!
Wash me in steep-down gulfs of liquid fire!

Antony and Cleopatra contains many examples of hyperbole. For example Cleopatra describes Antony:

His legs bestrid the ocean; his reared arm
Crested the world; his voice was propertied
As all the tunèd spheres, and that to friends;
But when he meant to quail and shake the orb,
He was as rattling thunder. For his bounty,
There was no winter in't; an autumn 'twas
That grew the more by reaping. His delights
Were dolphin-like; they showed his back above
The element they lived in. In his livery
Walked crowns and crownets; realms and islands were
As plates dropped from his pocket.

was propertied/As all
had all the qualities of

tunèd spheres
music of the heavens

orb
earth (his worldly enemies)

livery
service, uniform

crowns/crownets
kings/princes

plates
silver coins

In Love's Labour's Lost, Biron claims that 'A lover's eyes will gaze an eagle blind'.

1 Explore different ways of speaking Cleopatra's lines. In what ways might each of her descriptions be true?

2 Collect examples of hyperbole *either* in the play you are studying *or* in current advertisements in magazines and newspapers. Find an effective way of presenting your collection.

3 Make up a dozen lines of hyperbole to describe William Shakespeare, or one of his plays.

Hyperbole 2

USE WITH PAGE 52

Bassanio's description of Portia's portrait in *The Merchant of Venice* is an example of hyperbole ('hype'). It 'goes over the top', using elaborate and fanciful words, images, and styles.

counterfeit
portrait

bar
division

sunder
keep apart

unfurnished
without a companion

underprizing
not describing accurately

[Bassanio opens the leaden casket]

What find I here?
Fair Portia's counterfeit! What demi-god
Hath come so near creation? Move these eyes?
Or whether riding on the balls of mine
Seem they in motion? Here are severed lips
Parted with sugar breath; so sweet a bar
Should sunder such sweet friends. Here in her hairs
The painter plays the spider, and hath woven
A golden mesh t'entrap the hearts of men
Faster than gnats in cobwebs. But her eyes –
How could he see to do them? Having made one,
Methinks it should have power to steal both his
And leave itself unfurnished. Yet look how far
The substance of my praise doth wrong this shadow
In underprizing it, so far this shadow
Doth limp behind the substance.

1 Work in pairs. Take turns to speak the lines to each other, making them as extravagant or as persuasive as possible. Experiment with different ways of delivering the lines.

2 Taking a subject of your choice (for example, school food, a film star), make up a dozen lines that use exaggeration in a similar way to Bassanio.

Bombast

Bombast is boastful or ranting language. In *Henry IV part 1* Owen Glendower claims that when he was born 'The heavens were all on fire, the earth did tremble'. In *A Midsummer Night's Dream*, Bottom throws out his chest and declaims bombast:

> The raging rocks
> And shivering shocks
> Shall break the locks
> Of prison gates.

Hamlet uses similarly inflated language when he challenges Laertes and leaps into Ophelia's grave:

forbear him
leave him alone

'Swounds
by God's wounds

Woo't
would you (wilt thou)

eisel
vinegar

outface
outdo

prate
rant, bluster

our ground ... zone
the earth under our feet touches the sun

Ossa
mountain in Greece

HAMLET I loved Ophelia; forty thousand brothers
Could not with all their quantity of love
Make up my sum. What wilt thou do for her?
CLAUDIUS Oh he is mad Laertes.
GERTRUDE For love of God forbear him.
HAMLET 'Swounds, show me what thou't do.
Woo't weep, woo't fight, woo't fast, woo't tear thyself?
Woo't drink up eisel, eat a crocodile?
I'll do't Dost thou come here to whine,
To outface me with leaping in her grave?
Be buried quick with her, and so will I.
And if thou prate of mountains, let them throw
Millions of acres on us, till our ground,
Singeing his pate against the burning zone,
Make Ossa like a wart. Nay, and thou'lt mouth,
I'll rant as well as thou.

1 Speak Hamlet's lines as forcefully as you can. Pick out everything in them that makes them bombastic. What effect does bombast have on you? Find out about the context of the lines and suggest why you think Hamlet uses bombast at this moment.

2 Make up some lines of bombast of your own! See if you can outdo any Shakespeare character in boastful exaggeration.

Puns

The Elizabethans loved word play of all kinds, and puns were especially popular. When a word has two or more different meanings, the ambiguity can be used for witty effect, both comic and serious. The following examples are from *Love's Labour's Lost*, *Henry IV part 1*, *Othello*, and *Romeo and Juliet*:

ARMARDO By the North Pole, I do challenge thee.
COSTARD I will not fight with a pole, like a Northern man.

PISTOL To England will I steal, and there I'll steal.

OTHELLO *(carrying a candle, and about to kill Desdemona)*
Put out the light, and then put out the light.

MERCUTIO *(near to death, he cannot resist making a pun)*
Ask for me tomorrow, and you will find me a grave man.

In *The Taming of the Shrew*, Grumio deliberately misunderstands his master Petruchio's instruction to 'knock':

trow
believe, guess

rebused
insulted

pate
head

PETRUCHIO Verona, for a while I take my leave
To see my friends in Padua, but of all
My best belovèd and approvèd friend,
Hortensio: and I trow this is his house.
Here, sirrah Grumio, knock, I say.
GRUMIO Knock sir? Whom should I knock? Is there any man has rebused your worship?
PETRUCHIO Villain, I say, knock me here soundly.
GRUMIO Knock you here, sir? Why, sir, what am I, sir, that I should knock you here, sir?
PETRUCHIO Villain, I say, knock me at this gate,
And rap me well, or I'll knock your knave's pate!
GRUMIO My master is grown quarrelsome. I should knock you first,
And then I know after who comes by the worst.
PETRUCHIO Will it not be?
Faith, sirrah, and you'll not knock, I'll ring it.
I'll try how you can *sol-fa*, and sing it.

He wrings him by the ears.

GRUMIO Help, mistress, help! My master is mad.
PETRUCHIO Now knock when I bid you, sirrah villain.

1 Take parts as Grumio and Petruchio and speak their lines.

2 Some of Shakespeare's favourite punning words are 'light', 'dear', 'will' and 'lie'. Look up their meanings in a dictionary: how many definitions can you find for each word? Use some in a few lines of invented dialogue in which mistakes arise from puns.

Verbal irony, dramatic irony

USE WITH PAGE 57 OR 58

Verbal irony is in everyday use.

Shakespeare frequently uses these two types of irony. In both, the audience knows something that a character on stage does not.

Verbal irony: saying one thing but meaning another. For example, in *Julius Caesar*, Mark Antony repeatedly calls Brutus 'an honourable man' when he means quite the opposite.

Dramatic irony: what is said contrasts with what happens elsewhere in the play. The scene in which Macbeth plans to murder King Duncan is immediately followed by the unsuspecting Duncan praising the benign appearance of Macbeth's castle:

This castle hath a pleasant seat.

Dramatic irony: Romeo kills himself, unaware that Juliet is not really dead.

When a character uses irony intentionally, its purpose is usually to mock, to dissemble, or to mislead. Shakespeare's fondness for disguise, with women pretending to be men or characters hiding their real motives is a rich source of dramatic irony. Both Viola, disguised as a boy in *Twelfth Night,* and the villainous Iago in *Othello*, say 'I am not what I am'. Viola's irony has comic effect, Iago's is chilling.

1. Using the accompanying worksheet, pick out all the ambiguous words or phrases that give the lines ironic potential.
2. Irony is often conveyed by tone of voice or facial expression or gesture. An actor can make lines sound ironic. Practise speaking the lines on the accompanying worksheet with and without irony.
3. Collect examples of both verbal and dramatic irony from the play you are studying. Find a way of displaying or performing them to bring out their ironic effect.
4. The term 'irony' comes from Eiron, a clever underdog in ancient Greek comedy who always managed to come out on top by pretending to be stupid. Can you think of characters like this in modern films or television shows?

Irony: Juliet's ambiguous words

USE WITH PAGE 56

Lady Capulet thinks that Juliet is weeping for her cousin Tybalt, killed in a fight by Romeo. She does not know that Juliet loves Romeo, and has secretly married him.

asunder apart

runagate runaway

dram poison

temper mix, adjust

wreak avenge, bestow

LADY CAPULET Well, girl, thou weep'st not so much for his death
As that the villain lives which slaughtered him.
JULIET What villain, madam?
LADY CAPULET That same villain Romeo.
JULIET [*Aside*] Villain and he be many miles asunder.
God pardon him, I do with all my heart:
And yet no man like he doth grieve my heart.
LADY CAPULET That is because the traitor murderer lives.
JULIET Ay, madam, from the reach of these my hands.
Would none but I might venge my cousin's death!
LADY CAPULET We will have vengeance for it, fear thou not:
Then weep no more. I'll send to one in Mantua,
Where that same banished runagate doth live,
Shall give him such an unaccustomed dram
That he shall soon keep Tybalt company;
And then I hope thou wilt be satisfied.
JULIET Indeed I never shall be satisfied
With Romeo, till I behold him – dead –
Is my poor heart, so for a kinsman vexed.
Madam, if you could find out but a man
To bear a poison, I would temper it,
That Romeo should upon receipt thereof
Soon sleep in quiet. O how my heart abhors
To hear him named and cannot come to him,
To wreak the love I bore my cousin
Upon his body that hath slaughtered him!

1. Take parts and speak the lines. Have two persons playing Juliet. One speaks her lines with frequent pauses. In each pause, the other tells Juliet's true meaning.
2. How should Juliet speak? Suggest what tone of voice, expressions and movements she might make. On which lines might she make eye contact with her mother?
3. Invent a short piece of dialogue in which two people appear to be in complete agreement. In fact, the true meaning of one person's language is quite different from the other's.

Irony: Casca's ironic tone

USE WITH PAGE 56

Casca describes what happened when Julius Caesar was offered the crown to become supreme ruler of Rome.

fain
prefer to

chopped
chapped

swounded
fainted

doublet
Elizabethan jacket

man of any occupation
tradesman, man of action

infirmity
illness, weakness

I can as well be hanged as tell the manner of it. It was mere foolery, I did not mark it. I saw Mark Antony offer him a crown – yet 'twas not a crown neither, 'twas one of these coronets – and, as I told you, he put it by once; but for all that, to my thinking he would fain have had it. Then he offered it to him again; then he put it by again; but to my thinking he was very loath to lay his fingers off it. And then he offered it the third time; he put it the third time by, and still as he refused it, the rabblement hooted, and clapped their chopped hands, and threw up their sweaty nightcaps, and uttered such a deal of stinking breath because Caesar refused the crown that it had, almost, choked Caesar, for he swounded and fell down at it. And for mine own part I durst not laugh for fear of opening my lips and receiving the bad air ...

If the tag-rag people did not clap him and hiss him according as he pleased and displeased them, as they use to do the players in the theatre, I am no true man ...

Marry, before he fell down, when he perceived the common herd was glad he refused the crown, he plucked me ope his doublet and offered them his throat to cut. And I had been a man of any occupation, if I would not have taken him at a word I would I might go to hell among the rogues. And so he fell. When he came to himself again, he said if he had done or said anything amiss, he desired their worships to think it was his infirmity. Three or four wenches where I stood cried, 'Alas, good soul', and forgave him with all their hearts. But there's no heed to be taken of them: if Caesar had stabbed their mothers they would have done no less.

1. Casca's report is often spoken in an amused ironic tone, turning the solemn ceremony into comedy. Pick out all the opportunities the language provides for ironic humour or cynicism.
2. Speak the lines as ironically as possible, then try delivering them 'straight' as if Casca were giving a plain, objective account. Decide what style you think more suitable.
3. Write an account, in the same style as Casca, of a public occasion you have attended.

Oxymoron

Juliet, bidding farewell to Romeo, says:

Parting is such sweet sorrow

'Sweet sorrow' is an oxymoron: two incongruous or contradictory words brought together to make a striking expression. Much of Romeo and Juliet is about the clash of opposites: Montagues against Capulets, youth against age, life versus death, etc. Those oppositions are reflected in the oxymorons in the play:

ROMEO Here's much to do with hate, but more with love:
Why then, O brawling love, O loving hate,
O any thing of nothing first create!
O heavy lightness, serious vanity,
Misshapen chaos of well-seeming forms,
Feather of lead, bright smoke, cold fire, sick health,
Still-waking sleep, that is not what it is!

JULIET O serpent heart, hid with a flow'ring face!
Did ever dragon keep so fair a cave?
Beautiful tyrant, fiend angelical!
Dove-feathered raven, wolvish-ravening lamb!
Despisèd substance of divinest show!
Just opposite to what thou justly seem'st,
A damnèd saint, an honourable villain!

'Loving hate'

1 Work with a partner or small group. Choose one of Romeo's or Juliet's oxymorons (Romeo has a dozen oxymorons, Juliet has at least seven). Portray the oxymoron as a still photograph, or tableau. The class guesses which oxymoron has been chosen.

2 Make up oxymorons of your own and act them out for the class to guess. If you want a few 'starters', fill in the blanks:

slow ....

cowardly ....

Malapropism

Shakespeare created characters who mangle the English language with happy abandon. His clowns delighted in malapropisms: inappropriate, muddled or mistaken use of words. Malapropisms are named after Mrs Malaprop who muddled up similar-sounding words in Sheridan's play *The Rivals* (1775). In *King Henry IV Part 2*, Mistress Quickly, the Hostess of the Boar's Head Tavern, frequently uses malapropisms.

In *Much Ado About Nothing*, Dogberry and his deputy Verges set about appointing a constable to take charge of the Watch (local police):

give them their charge
explain their duties

stand
stop

DOGBERRY Are you good men and true?

VERGES Yea, or else it were pity but they should suffer salvation body and soul.

DOGBERRY Nay, that were a punishment too good for them, if they should have any allegiance in them, being chosen for the prince's watch.

VERGES Well, give them their charge, neighbour Dogberry.

DOGBERRY First, who think you the most desartless man to be constable?

WATCHMAN Hugh Oatcake, sir, or George Seacoal, for they can write and read.

DOGBERRY Come hither, neighbour Seacoal, God hath blessed you with a good name: to be a well-favoured man, is the gift of Fortune, but to write and read, comes by nature.

SEACOAL Both which, master constable –

DOGBERRY You have: I knew it would be your answer: well, for your favour, sir, why give God thanks, and make no boast of it, and for your writing and reading, let that appear when there is no need of such vanity: you are thought here to be the most senseless and fit man for the constable of the watch: therefore bear you the lantern: this is your charge, you shall comprehend all vagrom men, you are to bid any man stand, in the prince's name.

1 Act out the scene. What are Dogberry and Verge trying to say? Devise your own version of the lines in which other characters (for example, the Watchmen) find ways of correcting the mistakes of Dogberry and Verges.

2 Make up and perform a short scene of your own, filled with malapropisms.

Pronouns: you and thee

USE WITH PAGE 62

Don't be worried by Shakespeare's use of 'thee', 'thy', 'thine' and 'thou'. Although these old-fashioned expressions have now dropped out of use in English, in Shakespeare's time they were commonly used alongside 'you' and 'your'. Elizabethans switched from using one to the other depending on the social context – as is still the case in other European languages.

'Thou' could be friendly and familiar, but could also signify contempt for a social inferior. For example, in *Twelfth Night*, Sir Toby Belch advises Sir Andrew Aguecheek to use 'thou' as an insult.

'You' was usually a more formal, distant, respectful form of address.

When a character switches from one style to the other, it suggests a change of mood or attitude towards the other character. For example in *The Two Gentlemen of Verona*, Silvia rejects the advances of the deceitful Proteus, switching from 'you' to 'thou':

SILVIA What's your will?
PROTEUS That I may compass yours.
SILVIA You have your wish; my will is even this,
That presently you hie you home to bed.
Thou subtle, perjured, false, disloyal man,
Think'st thou I am so shallow, so conceitless,
To be seducèd by thy flattery,
That hast deceived so many with thy vows?
Return, return, and make thy love amends.
For me – by this pale queen of night I swear –
I am so far from granting thy request
That I despise thee for thy wrongful suit
And by and by intend to chide myself
Even for this time I spend in talking to thee.

will
wish (but Proteus interprets it as 'sexual desire')

compass
win, obtain

subtle
crafty

conceitless
unintelligent

pale queen of night
moon (Diana, goddess of chastity)

suit
wooing

chide
scold

1 Take parts as Silvia and Proteus. Speak the lines several times. Try to emphasise Silvia's use of 'thee', 'thou' and 'thy' to express her contempt for Proteus.

2 Turn at random to several pages of the Shakespeare play you are currently studying. Which pronouns do characters use? Why?

Pronouns: eternal triangle

USE WITH PAGE 61

In Sonnet 42 Shakespeare recounts how the woman he loves and his best friend, a young man, now love each other. He tries to console himself.

of my wailing chief
the major reason for my sorrow

touches
affects

nearly
deeply

Suff'ring
allowing

approve
seduce, love

both twain
both of you

cross
suffering (echoing the crucifixion of Jesus)

flattery
deception

That thou hast her, it is not all my grief,
And yet it may be said I loved her dearly:
That she hath thee is of my wailing chief,
A loss in love that touches me more nearly.
Loving offenders, thus I will excuse ye:
Thou dost love her because thou know'st I love her.
And for my sake even so doth she abuse me,
Suff'ring my friend for my sake to approve her.
If I lose thee, my loss is my love's gain,
And losing her, my friend hath found that loss;
Both find each other, and I lose both twain,
And both for my sake lay on me this cross.
  But here's the joy, my friend and I are one.
  Sweet flattery! then she loves but me alone.

Work in a group of three and take parts as Shakespeare, the young man and the woman. As Shakespeare slowly reads the sonnet aloud, everyone points emphatically to whoever is mentioned. There are well over forty such 'pointings'.

Pronouns: who's who?

At the end of the play, Friar Lawrence explains his part in the deaths of Romeo and Juliet.

doomsday
day of death

pined
grieve

perforce
by force

cell
room

stayed
detained

Romeo, there dead, was husband to that Juliet,
And she, there dead, that Romeo's faithful wife:
I married them, and their stol'n marriage day
Was Tybalt's doomsday, whose untimely death
Banished the new-made bridegroom from this city,
For whom, and not for Tybalt, Juliet pined.
You, to remove that siege of grief from her,
Betrothed and would have married her perforce
To County Paris. Then comes she to me,
And with wild looks bid me devise some mean
To rid her from this second marriage,
Or in my cell there would she kill herself.
Then gave I her (so tutored by my art)
A sleeping potion, which so took effect
As I intended, for it wrought on her
The form of death. Mean time I writ to Romeo
That he should hither come as this dire night
To help to take her from her borrowed grave,
Being the time the potion's force should cease.
But he which bore my letter, Friar John,
Was stayed by accident, and yesternight
Returned my letter back. Then all alone,
At the prefixèd hour of her waking,
Came I to take her from her kindred's vault,
Meaning to keep her closely at my cell,
Till I conveniently could send to Romeo.
But when I came, some minute ere the time
Of her awakening, here untimely lay
The noble Paris and true Romeo dead.
She wakes, and I entreated her come forth
And bear this work of heaven with patience.
But then a noise did scare me from the tomb,
And she too desperate would not go with me,
But as it seems, did violence on herself.

Take parts and stand in a circle. The parts are: Romeo, Juliet, Friar Lawrence, Friar John, Capulet, Paris, Tybalt. As Friar Lawrence slowly reads the lines, everyone points emphatically to whoever is mentioned in any way. How many 'points' can you find? To help you, the 'You' in the seventh line refers to Capulet, Juliet's father.

Changing language

Some words that Shakespeare used have changed their meaning since his time. In the following list, the meaning that Shakespeare probably had in mind is given in brackets.

silly (simple, homely, innocent)
luxurious (lustful)
still (always)
tell (count)
habit (dress, garment, clothes)
owe (own)
naughty (wicked, worthless)
fond (foolish)
marry (indeed)
sudden (violent)
neat (ox, cow)
let (hinder)
humour (temperament)
shrewd (unpleasant)
presently (immediately)
quick (alive, living)
several (separate)

Other words that Shakespeare used have dropped out of use altogether. Their meaning is given in brackets.

haply (perhaps)
eke (also)
hight (called)
perdy (by God)
inch-meal (inch by inch)
mocks and mows (insulting gestures and faces)
clepe (call)
hardiment (valour)
leman (sweetheart)
tristful (sad)
dole (sorrow)
hie (hasten)
wight (person)
yare (ready, nimble)

1 Use words from the first list above to invent a short dialogue between two characters. They constantly misunderstand each other because one uses the words in their modern sense, the other uses them in their Shakespeare meaning.

2 Make up a very short story that contains at least six of the words in the second list above. Try to make their meaning clear by their context.

Inventing words

USE WITH PAGE 66

Shakespeare wrote at a time when the English language was extremely fluid. Poets and playwrights felt free to make up words, to adapt old ones, and to change old meanings to new. If a word did not exist, Shakespeare used his dramatic imagination to remould an old one or make up a new one. He played with language to invent active, lively words to suit his dramatic purposes.

- He invented mock-Russian in *All's Well that Ends Well* for the ambush of Parolles:

  LORD DUMAINE Throca movousus, cargo, cargo, cargo.
  SOLDIERS Cargo, cargo, cargo, villianda par corbo, cargo.

- He made up nonsense words that seem to have meaning in context:

  skimble-skamble, hugger-mugger, hurly burly, kickie wickie, miching mallecho

- He made verbs out of adjectives (happies, bolds, gentle, pale) and nouns ('he childed as I fathered').

- He added prefixes such as un-, be-, en- and dis-.

  unkinged, unsex, uncaught, unhair, undeaf, unfathered, unpeople

  behowl, bespeak, bemock, bemoan, bemask, bedim

  discandy (dissolve, melt), disbench, disburden

  endanger, enthrall, engoal, enskied, entomb, entame, enwheel, encircle, enlist

---

Follow Shakespeare's practice! Use the examples above to help you make up words of your own by creating nonsense words, or by adding prefixes (un-, be-, en-, dis-). Give your new words a context by writing a short scene with characters who use such language.

Inventing words with the hyphen

USE WITH PAGE 65

Shakespeare uses the hyphen frequently to create compound words that conjure up vivid images, for example, tell-tale, love-sick, grim-looked, lack-brain. Such twofold words present exciting challenges to the imagination. Here are just a few from *The Tempest*:

wide-chopped	over-topping	O'er-prized
sea-sorrow	sea-swallowed	sight-outrunning
up-staring	still-vexed	pinch-spotted
hag-born	Side-stitches	brine-pits
Hag-seed	sea-change	Sea-nymphs
fresh-brook		

Few of these hyphenated words can be pinned down to a single, exact meaning. Shakespeare may have used them because their appeal to the imagination expresses the sense of wonder and ever-changing reality in the play.

In The Comedy of Errors, Doctor Pinch is described as a 'hollow-eyed, sharp-looking wretch'.

1 Create your own compound words using the hyphen. Use them to describe characters, events and actions in a short play of your own.

2 Find examples of hyphenated words in the play you are studying. Display them in an effective way.

Everyday language

If you say something smells to heaven, that you see something in your mind's eye or that something is a foregone conclusion, then you are speaking Shakespeare. These, and hundreds of other Shakespearean expressions, have become part of everyday language.

Here are just a few expressions from *Romeo and Juliet* that you can hear today. Listen out for them!

star-crossed lovers
parting is such sweet sorrow
last embrace
above compare
light of heart
past hope
in a fool's paradise
what's in a name?
what must be shall be
I will not budge
I know what
where have you been gadding?
I thought all for the best
let me alone
fortune's fool
leave to go
if love be blind
as true as steel
last farewell
cock-a-hoop
as gentle as a lamb
past help
on a wild goose chase
we were born to die
stiff and stark
on pain of death
in one short minute
the weakest go to the wall
go like lightning
my only love
a plague on both your houses
Where the devil?
a rose by any other word would smell as sweet

1. Use as many of the above expressions as you can to make up a short story.
2. Search through the play you are currently studying to find familiar expressions that people still use today. Find an appropriate way of presenting them actively.

Dialogue

USE WITH ONE OF PAGES 69 TO 76

There are dialogues of all kinds in Shakespeare's plays: the tender exchange of love between Romeo and Juliet in the balcony scene: Romeo and Mercutio joking together; Friar Lawrence advising the young lovers; Romeo's brief but bloody encounter with Paris outside the tomb of the Capulets, and so on. Every exchange has its different tones, rhythms and moods.

Dialogue is verbal exchange between two or more characters. For example, in *Hamlet,* Shakespeare uses the technique of rapidly alternating single lines (stichomythia). Hamlet and his mother respond to each other's words in a head on clash, each intensely sensitive to the other's thoughts and feelings:

> HAMLET Now mother, what's the matter?
> GERTRUDE Hamlet, thou hast thy father much offended.
> HAMLET Mother, you have my father much offended.
> GERTRUDE Come, come, you answer with an idle tongue.
> HAMLET Go, go, you question with a wicked tongue.

But when four lovers echo each other in As *You Like It*, the effect is quite different, more like a chorus than a conversation. Each character seems to be speaking more to himself or herself than developing a dialogue:

> PHOEBE Good shepherd, tell this youth what 'tis to love
> SILVIUS It is to be all made of sighs and tears,
> And so am I for Phoebe.
> PHOEBE And I for Ganymede.
> ORLANDO And I for Rosalind.
> ROSALIND And I for no woman.

---

1 In the play you are currently studying, follow a character through the play. How much does the character switch language style in different dialogues?

2 Use the accompanying worksheet. Take parts and speak the exchange several times.

   a Identify the features which suggest the characters are really listening and responding to each other, or not! Is there a 'leader' in the conversation, or are all speakers 'equal'?

   b Suggest how each exchange might be staged to greatest dramatic effect: changes in mood, tone of voice, pace, pauses, movement around the stage, gestures and facial expressions, etc.

   c From this brief extract what can you deduce about each character's motivations and personality, and the relationships of the characters?

3 Try your hand at writing dialogue. Choose any two Shakespeare characters, or one Shakespearean and one modern soap opera character, invent a meeting and write what they might say to each other.

Dialogue: in the graveyard

USE WITH PAGE 68

Prince Hamlet, in the company of Horatio, questions a gravedigger (Clown), but does not get straight answers.

quick
living

absolute
precise, literal

by the card
accurately (like a sailor with a compass card)

equivocation
deliberate ambiguity, double meaning

picked his kibe
scuffs his chilblain (treads on his heels)

HAMLET Whose grave's this sirrah?

CLOWN Mine sir.

[Sings]

Oh a pit of clay for to be made
For such a guest is meet.

HAMLET I think it be thine indeed, for thou liest in't.

CLOWN You lie out on't sir, and therefore 'tis not yours. For my part, I do not lie in't, yet it is mine.

HAMLET Thou dost lie in't, to be in't and say 'tis thine. 'Tis for the dead, not for the quick, therefore thou liest.

CLOWN 'Tis a quick lie sir, 'twill away again from me to you.

HAMLET What man dost thou dig it for?

CLOWN For no man sir.

HAMLET What woman then?

CLOWN For none neither.

HAMLET Who is to be buried in't?

CLOWN One that was a woman sir, but rest her soul she's dead.

HAMLET How absolute the knave is! We must speak by the card, or equivocation will undo us. By the lord, Horatio, this three years I have took note of it: the age is grown so picked, that the toe of the peasant comes so near the heel of the courtier, he galls his kibe. How long hast thou been grave-maker?

CLOWN Of all the days i'th'year, I came to't that day that our last King Hamlet o'ercame Fortinbras.

HAMLET How long is that since?

CLOWN Cannot you tell that? Every fool can tell that. It was the very day that young Hamlet was born, he that is mad and sent into England.

HAMLET Ay marry, why was he sent into England?

CLOWN Why, because a was mad. A shall recover his wits there, or if a do not, 'tis no great matter there.

HAMLET Why?

CLOWN 'Twill not be seen in him there. There the men are as mad as he.

Use with Activity 2a–c on page 68.

Dialogue: after the murder

USE WITH PAGE 68

It is shortly after midnight. Macbeth has just murdered Duncan. He returns to the waiting Lady Macbeth. His conscience strikes.

Enter MACBETH *[with two bloody daggers]*

they have awaked
(Duncan's bodyguards)

Consider it not so deeply
don't brood on it

MACBETH Who's there? What ho?
LADY MACBETH Alack, I am afraid they have awaked,
And 'tis not done; th'attempt and not the deed
Confounds us – hark – I laid their daggers ready,
He could not miss 'em. Had he not resembled
My father as he slept, I had done't. My husband?
MACBETH I have done the deed. Didst thou not hear a noise?
LADY MACBETH I heard the owl scream and the crickets cry.
Did not you speak?
MACBETH When?
LADY MACBETH Now.
MACBETH As I descended?
LADY MACBETH Ay.
MACBETH Hark, who lies i'th'second chamber?
LADY MACBETH Donaldbain.
MACBETH This is a sorry sight.
LADY MACBETH A foolish thought, to say a sorry sight.
MACBETH There's one did laugh in's sleep, and one cried, 'Murder!',
That they did wake each other; I stood, and heard them,
But they did say their prayers and addressed them
Again to sleep.
LADY MACBETH There are two lodged together.
MACBETH One cried 'God bless us!' and 'Amen' the other,
As they had seen me with these hangman's hands.
List'ning their fear, I could not say 'Amen'
When they did say 'God bless us.'
LADY MACBETH Consider it not so deeply.
MACBETH But wherefore could not I pronounce 'Amen'?
I had most need of blessing and 'Amen'
Stuck in my throat.
LADY MACBETH These deeds must not be thought
After these ways; so, it will make us mad.

Use with Activity 2a–c on page 68.

Dialogue: what need one?

USE WITH PAGE 68

King Lear has given everything to his daughters, keeping only one hundred knights for himself. But his daughters, Regan and Gonerill, are not satisfied.

looked not for
did not expect

I dare avouch it
it is true

sith
since

Hold amity
live in friendship

slack ye
serve you badly

depositaries
inheritors, trustees

stands in some rank
deserves, merits

LEAR I can be patient, I can stay with Regan,
I and my hundred knights.
REGAN Not altogether so.
I looked not for you yet, nor am provided
For your fit welcome. Give ear, sir, to my sister,
For those that mingle reason with your passion
Must be content to think you old, and so –
But she knows what she does.
LEAR Is this well spoken?
REGAN I dare avouch it, sir. What, fifty followers?
Is it not well? What should you need of more?
Yea, or so many, sith that both charge and danger
Speak 'gainst so great a number? How in one house
Should many people under two commands
Hold amity? 'Tis hard, almost impossible.
GONERILL Why might not you, my lord, receive attendance
From those that she calls servants, or from mine?
REGAN Why not, my lord? If then they chanced to slack ye,
We could control them. If you will come to me
(For now I spy a danger) I entreat you
To bring but five and twenty; to no more
Will I give place or notice.
LEAR I gave you all.
REGAN And in good time you gave it.
LEAR Made you my guardians, my depositaries,
But kept a reservation to be followed
With such a number. What, must I come to you
With five and twenty? Regan, said you so?
REGAN And speak't again, my lord. No more with me.
LEAR Those wicked creatures yet do look well-favoured
When others are more wicked. Not being the worst
Stands in some rank of praise. [*To Gonerill*] I'll go with thee;
Thy fifty yet doth double five and twenty,
And thou art twice her love.
GONERILL Hear me, my lord:
What need you five and twenty? ten? or five?
To follow in a house where twice so many
Have a command to tend you?
REGAN What need one?

1 Use with Activity 2a–c on page 68.

2 Work out how the scene builds up to the climax of 'What need one?'

Dialogue: Beatrice and Benedick

USE WITH PAGE 68

In *Much Ado About Nothing*, Beatrice is distressed that Claudio has falsely accused her cousin of unfaithfulness and has refused to marry her. Benedick, Claudio's friend, tries to comfort her.

office
duty, task

stayed me in a happy hour
given support at a fortunate moment

BENEDICK Lady Beatrice, have you wept all this while?
BEATRICE Yea, and I will weep a while longer.
BENEDICK I will not desire that.
BEATRICE You have no reason, I do it freely.
BENEDICK Surely I do believe your fair cousin is wronged.
BEATRICE Ah, how much might the man deserve of me that would right her!
BENEDICK Is there any way to show such friendship?
BEATRICE A very even way, but no such friend.
BENEDICK May a man do it?
BEATRICE It is a man's office, but not yours.
BENEDICK I do love nothing in the world so well as you, is not that strange?
BEATRICE As strange as the thing I know not: it were as possible for me to say, I loved nothing so well as you, but believe me not, and yet I lie not, I confess nothing, nor I deny nothing: I am sorry for my cousin.
BENEDICK By my sword, Beatrice, thou lovest me.
BEATRICE Do not swear and eat it.
BENEDICK I will swear by it that you love me, and I will make him eat it that says I love not you.
BEATRICE Will you not eat your word?
BENEDICK With no sauce that can be devised to it: I protest I love thee.
BEATRICE Why then God forgive me.
BENEDICK What offence, sweet Beatrice?
BEATRICE You have stayed me in a happy hour, I was about to protest I loved you.
BENEDICK And do it with all thy heart.
BEATRICE I love you with so much of my heart, that none is left to protest.
BENEDICK Come bid me do anything for thee.
BEATRICE Kill Claudio.

Beatrice and Benedick have verbally fenced with each other many times in the past. Now they reveal their true feelings for each other, and their wordplay becomes much more serious.

1 Use with Activity 2a–c on page 68.

2 'Kill Claudio' has been spoken on stage in dozens of different ways. Explore five or six possibilities together with accompanying actions.

Dialogue: conversation or duet?

USE WITH PAGE 68

In *A Midsummer Night's Dream* Hermia and Lysander regret the difficulties and brevity of love.

Beteem
grant

aught
anything

blood
class, family background

enthralled
bound, in love with

misgraffèd
mismatched

momentany
momentary, short-lived

collied
dark

spleen
burst of temper

LYSANDER How now, my love? Why is your cheek so pale?
How chance the roses there do fade so fast?
HERMIA Belike for want of rain, which I could well
Beteem them from the tempest of my eyes.
LYSANDER Ay me! For aught that I could ever read,
Could ever hear by tale or history,
The course of true love never did run smooth;
But either it was different in blood –
HERMIA O cross! too high to be enthralled to low.
LYSANDER Or else misgraffèd in respect of years –
HERMIA O spite! too old to be engaged to young.
LYSANDER Or else it stood upon the choice of friends –
HERMIA O hell, to choose love by another's eyes!
LYSANDER Or, if there were a sympathy in choice,
War, death, or sickness did lay siege to it,
Making it momentany as a sound,
Swift as a shadow, short as any dream,
Brief as the lightning in the collied night,
That in a spleen unfolds both heaven and earth,
And, ere a man hath power to say 'Behold!',
The jaws of darkness do devour it up.
So quick bright things come to confusion.

1 Use with Activity 2a–c on page 68.

2 Hermia and Lysander's dialogue has been likened to a formal and rhythmical musical duet. Try speaking it in such a way, then speak it as an informal conversation.

3 Act out the six obstacles to true love described. They run from 'different in blood' to 'sickness'.

Dialogue: eat up your leeks!

USE WITH PAGE 68

In *King Henry V*, Llewellyn, a Welsh captain, gets his revenge on Pistol.

Cadwallader legendary Welsh king

scald scurvy, scabby

victuals food

Chesu Jesus

green fresh

groat fourpence

cudgels clubs

LLEWELLYN I peseech you heartily, scurvy, lousy knave, at my desires and my requests and my petitions, to eat, look you, this leek. Because, look you, you do not love it, nor your affections and your appetites and your digestions does not agree with it, I would desire you to eat it.

PISTOL Not for Cadwallader and all his goats.

LLEWELLYN There is one goat for you.

Strikes him [with cudgel]

Will you be so good, scald knave, as eat it?

PISTOL Base Trojan, thou shalt die!

LLEWELLYN You say very true, scald knave, when God's will is. I will desire you to live in the meantime, and eat your victuals. Come, there is sauce for it. [*Strikes him*] You called me yesterday 'mountain-squire', but I will make you today a squire of low degree. I pray you, fall to. If you can mock a leek, you can eat a leek.

GOWER Enough captain. You have astonished him.

LLEWELLYN By Cheshu, I will make him eat some part of my leek, or I will peat his pate four days. Bite, I pray you. It is good for your green wound, and your ploody coxcomb.

PISTOL Must I bite?

LLEWELLYN Yes, certainly, and out of doubt and out of question too, and ambiguities.

PISTOL By this leek, I will most horribly revenge – [*Llewellyn threatens him*] I eat and eat, I swear!

LLEWELLYN Eat, I pray you. Will you have some more sauce to your leek? There is not enough leek to swear by.

PISTOL Quiet thy cudgel, thou dost see I eat.

LLEWELLYN Much good do you, scald knave, heartily. Nay, pray you throw none away. The skin is good for your broken coxcomb. When you take occasions to see leeks hereafter, I pray you mock at 'em, that is all.

PISTOL Good.

LLEWELLYN Ay, leeks is good. Hold you, there is a groat to heal your pate.

PISTOL Me a groat?

LLEWELLYN Yes, verily, and in truth you shall take it, or I have another leek in my pocket which you shall eat.

PISTOL I take thy groat in earnest of revenge.

LLEWELLYN If I owe you anything, I will pay you in cudgels. You shall be a woodmonger, and buy nothing of me but cudgels. God b'wi' you, and keep you, and heal your pate.

Use with Activity 2a–c on page 68.

Dialogue: Hamlet and Claudius

USE WITH PAGE 68

Claudius questions Hamlet about Polonius, who has just been killed by Hamlet. Claudius has planned to send Hamlet abroad to be executed in England.

fat all creatures else
feed farm animals

variable service
different dishes in a menu

progress
royal procession

i'th'other place
in Hell

A will stay till you come
he won't move

do tender
have concern for

bark
ship

Th'associates tend
your servants (or bodyguards) are ready

mother
(Claudius has married Hamlet's mother)

CLAUDIUS Now Hamlet, where's Polonius?

HAMLET At supper.

CLAUDIUS At supper? Where?

HAMLET Not where he eats, but where a is eaten. A certain convocation of politic worms are e'en at him. Your worm is your only emperor for diet: we fat all creatures else to fat us, and we fat ourselves for maggots. Your fat king and your lean beggar is but variable service, two dishes, but to one table; that's the end.

CLAUDIUS Alas, alas.

HAMLET A man may fish with the worm that hath eat of a king, and eat of the fish that hath fed of that worm.

CLAUDIUS What dost thou mean by this?

HAMLET Nothing but to show you how a king may go a progress through the guts of a beggar.

CLAUDIUS Where is Polonius?

HAMLET In heaven, send thither to see. If your messenger find him not there, seek him i'th'other place yourself. But if indeed you find him not within this month, you shall nose him as you go up the stairs into the lobby.

CLAUDIUS Go seek him there.

HAMLET A will stay till you come.

[Exeunt Attendants]

CLAUDIUS Hamlet, this deed, for thine especial safety,
Which we do tender, as we dearly grieve
For that which thou hast done, must send thee hence
With fiery quickness. Therefore prepare thyself.
The bark is ready and the wind at help,
Th'associates tend, and everything is bent
For England.

HAMLET For England?

CLAUDIUS Ay Hamlet.

HAMLET Good.

CLAUDIUS So is it if thou knew'st our purposes.

HAMLET I see a cherub that sees them. But come, for England! Farewell dear mother.

CLAUDIUS Thy loving father, Hamlet.

HAMLET My mother. Father and mother is man and wife, man and wife is one flesh, and so, my mother. Come, for England. *Exit*

Use with Activity 2a–c on page 68.

Dialogue: a sexist portrayal?

USE WITH PAGE 68

In *The Comedy of Errors* Dromio describes Nell:

rags
clothes

tallow
grease

swart
black

ell
forty-five inches (about 1.14m)

armed and reverted … heir
a reference to the civil war in France, and a pun on 'hair'

armadoes of carracks
armadas of merchant ships

DROMIO Marry, sir, she's the kitchen wench, and all grease; and I know not what use to put her to but to make a lamp of her and run from her by her own light. I warrant her rags and the tallow in them will burn a Poland winter. If she lives till doomsday she'll burn a week longer than the whole world.

ANTIPHOLUS What complexion is she of?

DROMIO Swart like my shoe, but her face nothing like so clean kept. For why? She sweats a man may go overshoes in the grime of it.

ANTIPHOLUS That's a fault that water will mend.

DROMIO No, sir, 'tis in grain. Noah's flood could not do it.

ANTIPHOLUS What's her name?

DROMIO Nell, sir. But her name and three quarters – that's an ell and three quarters – will not measure her from hip to hip.

ANTIPHOLUS Then she bears some breadth?

DROMIO No longer from head to foot than from hip to hip. She is spherical, like a globe; I could find out countries in her.

ANTIPHOLUS In what part of her body stands Ireland?

DROMIO Marry, sir, in her buttocks. I found it out by the bogs.

ANTIPHOLUS Where Scotland?

DROMIO I found it by the barrenness, hard in the palm of the hand.

ANTIPHOLUS Where France?

DROMIO In her forehead, armed and reverted, making war against her heir.

ANTIPHOLUS Where England?

DROMIO I looked for the chalky cliffs, but I could find no whiteness in them. But I guess it stood in her chin, by the salt rheum that ran between France and it.

ANTIPHOLUS Where Spain?

DROMIO Faith, I saw it not, but I felt it hot in her breath.

ANTIPHOLUS Where America, the Indies?

DROMIO O, sir, upon her nose, all o'er embellished with rubies, carbuncles, sapphires, declining their rich aspect to the hot breath of Spain, who sent whole armadoes of carracks to be ballast at her nose.

ANTIPHOLUS Where stood Belgia, the Netherlands?

DROMIO O, sir, I did not look so low.

---

1 Write a description of a man, likening his appearance to different countries. Use an atlas to help you.

2 Some people find this passage sexist and chauvinist, showing contempt for women and other nations in its stereotyping. How would you justify it in a stage performance?

3 Use with activity 2a–c on page 68.

Soliloquy

USE WITH ONE OF PAGES 78 TO 84

If you saw someone in the street talking to himself or herself, what would you do? Many people would cross over to the other side to avoid contact. In real life someone who talks to himself or herself is often thought to be odd. But in a Shakespeare play, such behaviour is an accepted convention.

A soliloquy is a kind of internal debate spoken by a character who is alone on stage, or who believes himself or herself to be alone.

The stage convention assumes that characters tell the truth in soliloquy. A soliloquy reveals inner thought and feelings and so discloses what that character is really like. In *Richard III*, for example, the deceitful Richard declares his true nature to the audience in his first soliloquy – 'I am determined to prove a villain' – but until he becomes king, puts on a false face when he is with other characters. Iago, alone on stage, declares his hatred for Othello, but speaks as if he were an honest and faithful officer when he speaks to Othello.

Use some of the following suggestions to help you work on the soliloquy on the accompanying worksheet:

a Walk around the room reading the lines aloud. At every new thought, or at each punctuation mark, change direction.

b Work with a partner or in a small group and take turns to speak, for example, as a face-to-face conversation, or a telephone conversation.

c Carry out some repetitive physical activity as you speak the soliloquy, for example, painting a wall, counting money, bricklaying, ironing, bouncing a ball, walking on a tightrope.

d Experiment with speaking a soliloquy aloud to the following: the audience, the character himself or herself, an absent character, a god, heaven or hell, a real or imaginary object.

e What is the character like? Suggest what the soliloquy reveals about the character's nature, mood and attitude.

f Identify the imagery, antitheses, repetitions, lists and other language devices that the soliloquy uses to increase dramatic effect.

g How might the soliloquy be spoken on stage to heighten dramatic effect? Prepare a presentation of the soliloquy, writing notes on tone of voice, emphasis, gesture, movement, facial expression and so on. Deliver your version of the soliloquy to the class as if you were auditioning for a place at drama school.

h Step into role as a Shakespeare character of your choice and write a soliloquy for him or her, sharing with the audience the character's true thoughts, feelings, motivations and intentions.

Soliloquy: a guilty conscience

USE WITH PAGE 77

It is daybreak, shortly before the battle of Bosworth. King Richard III awakes from a terrible dream in which the ghosts of those he has killed come back to accuse him.

several
different

Perjury
false witness

direst
most dreadful

degree
level of criminality

Throng to the bar
come to the courtroom

Give me another horse! Bind up my wounds!
Have mercy, Jesu! – Soft! I did but dream.
O coward conscience, how dost thou afflict me!
The lights burn blue. It is now dead midnight.
Cold fearful drops stand on my trembling flesh.
What do I fear? Myself? There's none else by.
Richard loves Richard: that is, I am I.
Is there a murderer here? No. Yes, I am.
Then fly. What, from myself? Great reason why –
Lest I revenge. Myself upon myself?
Alack, I love myself. Wherefore? For any good
That I myself have done unto myself?
O no! Alas, I rather hate myself
For hateful deeds committed by myself.
I am a villain. Yet I lie, I am not.
Fool, of thyself speak well. Fool, do not flatter.
My conscience hath a thousand several tongues,
And every tongue brings in a several tale,
And every tale condemns me for a villain.
Perjury, perjury, in the highest degree.
Murder, stern murder, in the direst degree,
All several sins, all used in each degree,
Throng to the bar, crying all 'Guilty! Guilty!'
I shall despair. There is no creature loves me;
And if I die, no soul will pity me.
Nay, wherefore should they, since that I myself
Find in myself no pity to myself?
Methought the souls of all that I had murdered
Came to my tent, and every one did threat
Tomorrow's vengeance on the head of Richard.

Prepare a presentation of the soliloquy using suggestions a–g on page 77. Notice that Richard's soliloquy is filled with short sentences. In pairs or small groups, speak them in turn as an agonised conversation.

Soliloquy: 'To be, or not to be'

USE WITH PAGE 77

As the play approaches its halfway point, Hamlet reflects on death and the fear of death.

consummation
ending

rub
obstacle

shuffled off ...coil
died

contumely
humiliating insults

disprized
unvalued

office
people in authority

quietus
release

a bare bodkin
a mere dagger

fardels
burdens

native hue of resolution
natural determination to act

sicklied o'er
unhealthily covered

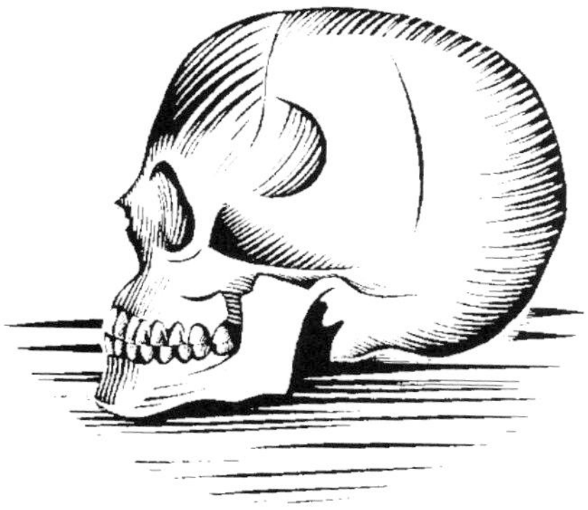

To be, or not to be, that is the question –
Whether 'tis nobler in the mind to suffer
The slings and arrows of outrageous fortune,
Or to take arms against a sea of troubles,
And by opposing end them. To die, to sleep –
No more; and by a sleep to say we end
The heart-ache and the thousand natural shocks
That flesh is heir to – 'tis a consummation
Devoutly to be wished. To die, to sleep –
To sleep, perchance to dream. Ay, there's the rub,
For in that sleep of death what dreams may come,
When we have shuffled off this mortal coil,
Must give us pause. There's the respect
That makes calamity of so long life,
For who would bear the whips and scorns of time,
Th'oppressor's wrong, the proud man's contumely,
The pangs of disprized love, the law's delay,
The insolence of office, and the spurns
That patient merit of th'unworthy takes,
When he himself might his quietus make
With a bare bodkin? Who would fardels bear,
To grunt and sweat under a weary life,
But that the dread of something after death,
The undiscovered country from whose bourn
No traveller returns, puzzles the will,
And makes us rather bear those ills we have
Than fly to others that we know not of?
Thus conscience does make cowards of us all,
And thus the native hue of resolution
Is sicklied o'er with the pale cast of thought,
And enterprises of great pitch and moment
With this regard their currents turn awry
And lose the name of action.

Prepare a presentation of the soliloquy using suggestions a–g on page 77.

Soliloquy: a dog misbehaves

USE WITH PAGE 77

In *The Two Gentlemen of Verona*, Lance tells how he was punished for the misdeeds of his dog, Crab.

went to it
were drowned

trencher
wooden plate

capon
chicken

keep himself
behave himself

all in the chamber
everyone in the room

wot
know

farthingale
long wide skirt supported on a frame

[*Pointing at his dog*] When a man's servant shall play the cur with him, look you, it goes hard – one that I brought up of a puppy, one that I saved from drowning when three or four of his blind brothers and sisters went to it. I have taught him, even as one would say precisely, 'Thus I would teach a dog.' I was sent to deliver him as a present to Mistress Silvia from my master; and I came no sooner into the dining-chamber but he steps me to her trencher and steals her capon's leg. O, 'tis a foul thing when a cur cannot keep himself in all companies. I would have, as one should say, one that takes upon him to be a dog indeed, to be, as it were, a dog at all things. If I had not had more wit than he, to take a fault upon me that he did, I think verily he had been hanged for't; sure as I live, he had suffered for't. You shall judge. He thrusts me himself into the company of three or four gentlemenlike dogs under the duke's table. He had not been there, bless the mark, a pissing while but all the chamber smelt him. 'Out with the dog', says one; 'What cur is that?', says another; 'Whip him out', says the third; 'Hang him up', says the duke. I, having been acquainted with the smell before, knew it was Crab, and goes me to the fellow that whips the dogs. 'Friend', quoth I, 'you mean to whip the dog?' 'Ay, marry, do I', quoth he. 'You do him the more wrong', quoth I, ' 'twas I did the thing you wot of.' He makes me no more ado but whips me out of the chamber. How many masters would do this for his servant? Nay, I'll be sworn I have sat in the stocks for puddings he hath stolen, otherwise he had been executed. I have stood on the pillory for geese he hath killed, otherwise he had suffered for't [*To his dog*] Thou think'st not of this now. Nay, I remember the trick you served me when I took my leave of Madam Silvia. Did not I bid thee still mark me and do as I do? When didst thou see me heave up my leg and make water against a gentlewoman's farthingale? Didst thou ever see me do such a trick?

Work in a group and use some of suggestions a–g on page 77 to help you devise your own presentation of Lance's soliloquy. You may decide to present it as a speech for many voices, or as it might be performed on stage by one person. Whatever method you decide, don't forget Crab! One person can play Crab, remembering the old saying that actors use 'Never work with children or animals. They always misbehave!'

Soliloquy: Juliet longs for Romeo

USE WITH PAGE 77

Phoebus' lodging
the west (where the sun sets)

Phoebus
the sun god

Phaëton
son of Phoebus who drove his father's chariot (the sun) so recklessly that Zeus, king of the gods, killed him with a thunderbolt

stainless
innocent

'Hood my unmanned blood, bating in my cheeks, with thy black mantle': an untrained hawk, unused to men ('unmanned'), fluttered its wings ('bating') until it was hooded with a black cap ('mantle').

Juliet, newly married to Romeo and filled with love for him, longs for night to come.

Gallop apace, you fiery-footed steeds,
Towards Phoebus' lodging; such a waggoner
As Phaëton would whip you to the west,
And bring in cloudy night immediately.
Spread thy close curtain, love-performing Night,
That runaways' eyes may wink, and Romeo
Leap to these arms, untalked of and unseen:
Lovers can see to do their amorous rites
By their own beauties, or if love be blind,
It best agrees with night. Come, civil Night,
Thou sober-suited matron all in black,
And learn me how to lose a winning match,
Played for a pair of stainless maidenhoods.
Hood my unmanned blood, bating in my cheeks,
With thy black mantle, till strange love grow bold,
Think true love acted simple modesty.
Come, Night, come, Romeo, come, thou day in night,
For thou wilt lie upon the wings of night,
Whiter than new snow upon a raven's back.
Come, gentle Night, come, loving, black-browed Night,
Give me my Romeo, and when I shall die,
Take him and cut him out in little stars,
And he will make the face of heaven so fine
That all the world will be in love with night,
And pay no worship to the garish sun.
O, I have bought the mansion of a love,
But not possessed it, and though I am sold,
Not yet enjoyed. So tedious is this day
As is the night before some festival
To an impatient child that hath new robes
And may not wear them.

1 Prepare a presentation of the soliloquy using suggestions a–g on page 77.

2 Juliet's language conveys the longing she feels for time to pass swiftly and bring Romeo to her. Her soliloquy is filled with commands and words that signify speed and time. To experience her urgent sense of impatient desire, emphasise every command or word concerned with speed or haste, for example, 'Gallop apace', 'fiery-footed', 'whip', etc.

Soliloquy: 'Is this a dagger?'

USE WITH PAGE 77

Macbeth, resolved to kill Duncan, hallucinates, thinking he sees a dagger.

sensible to feeling
able to be touched

heat-oppressèd
feverish

palpable
real, physical

marshall'st
lead, point

dudgeon
handle

gouts
large drops

Hecate
goddess of witchcraft

sentinel
sentry, guard

Tarquin
Roman prince who raped Lucrece

prate
talk

Is this a dagger which I see before me,
The handle toward my hand? Come, let me clutch thee:
I have thee not, and yet I see thee still.
Art thou not, fatal vision, sensible
To feeling as to sight? Or art thou but
A dagger of the mind, a false creation,
Proceeding from the heat-oppressèd brain?
I see thee yet, in form as palpable
As this which now I draw.
Thou marshall'st me the way that I was going,
And such an instrument I was to use.
Mine eyes are made the fools o'th'other senses,
Or else worth all the rest. I see thee still
And on thy blade and dudgeon gouts of blood,
Which was not so before. There's no such thing:
It is the bloody business which informs
Thus to mine eyes. Now o'er the one half-world
Nature seems dead, and wicked dreams abuse
The curtained sleep. Witchcraft celebrates
Pale Hecate's off'rings, and withered murder,
Alarumed by his sentinel, the wolf,
Whose howl's his watch, thus with his stealthy pace,
With Tarquin's ravishing strides, towards his design
Moves like a ghost. Thou sure and firm-set earth,
Hear not my steps, which way they walk, for fear
Thy very stones prate of my whereabout,
And take the present horror from the time,
Which now suits with it. Whiles I threat, he lives;
Words to the heat of deeds too cold breath gives.

A bell rings

I go, and it is done. The bell invites me.
Hear it not, Duncan, for it is a knell
That summons thee to heaven or to hell.

The soliloquy is filled with built-in stage directions and vivid imagery. The alternating questions, commands and emphatic statements at the start show the conflicts in Macbeth's mind as he struggles to make sense of what he 'sees'. Explore ways of presenting the soliloquy using suggestions a–g on page 77.

Soliloquy: renouncing magic

USE WITH PAGE 77

In *The Tempest*, Prospero prepares to give up his magic powers.

ebbing Neptune
retreating tide

demi-puppets
tiny spirits

green sour ringlets
'fairy rings' in grass

solemn curfew
bell that signals night has come

azured vault
blue sky

rifted
split

bolt
thunderbolt

spurs
roots

airy charms
music

Ye elves of hills, brooks, standing lakes, and groves,
And ye that on the sands with printless foot
Do chase the ebbing Neptune, and do fly him
When he comes back; you demi-puppets, that
By moon-shine do the green sour ringlets make,
Whereof the ewe not bites; and you, whose pastime
Is to make midnight mushrooms, that rejoice
To hear the solemn curfew; by whose aid –
Weak masters though ye be – I have bedimmed
The noontide sun, called forth the mutinous winds,
And 'twixt the green sea and the azured vault
Set roaring war. To the dread rattling thunder
Have I given fire, and rifted Jove's stout oak
With his own bolt; the strong-based promontory
Have I made shake, and by the spurs plucked up
The pine and cedar; graves at my command
Have waked their sleepers, oped, and let 'em forth
By my so potent art. But this rough magic
I here abjure. And when I have required
Some heavenly music – which even now I do –
To work mine end upon their senses that
This airy charm is for, I'll break my staff,
Bury it certain fathoms in the earth,
And deeper than did ever plummet sound
I'll drown my book.

Prospero's lines are a kind of invocation or spell, appealing to magical forces and declaring that he will give up his supernatural powers. Use suggestions a–g on page 77 to prepare a presentation that brings out the soliloquy's spell-like qualities.

Soliloquy: the sleepless king

USE WITH PAGE 77

King Henry IV reflects that the ordinary people in his kingdom are sleeping soundly, whilst he is unable to find comfort in sleep.

steep
saturate, soak

smoky cribs
chimneyless hovels

uneasy pallets
uncomfortable straw beds

canopies of costly state
expensive bed-curtains (like those on a four-poster bed)

watch-case
sentry box, watchman's hut

'larum bell
alarm bell (that prevents sleep)

billows
waves

deafing
deafening

hurly
confusion

partial
biased, favouring

means to boot
facilities also

low
low status people

How many thousand of my poorest subjects
Are at this hour asleep? O Sleep! O gentle Sleep!
Nature's soft nurse, how have I frighted thee,
That thou no more wilt weigh my eye-lids down
And steep my senses in forgetfulness?
Why rather Sleep liest thou in smoky cribs,
Upon uneasy pallets stretching thee
And hushed with buzzing night-flies to thy slumber,
Than in the perfumed chambers of the great,
Under the canopies of costly state
And lulled with sound of sweetest melody?
O thou dull god, why liest thou with the vile,
In loathsome beds, and leavest the kingly couch
A watch-case, or a common 'larum bell?
Wilt thou upon the high and giddy mast
Seal up the ship-boy's eyes and rock his brains
In cradle of the rude imperious surge
And in the visitation of the winds,
Who take the ruffian billows by the top,
Curling their monstrous heads and hanging them
With deafing clamour in the slippery clouds,
That, with the hurly, death itself awakes?
Canst thou, O partial Sleep, give thy repose
To the wet sea-son in an hour so rude,
And, in the calmest and most stillest night
With all appliances and means to boot,
Deny it to a king? Then happy low lie down,
Uneasy lies the head that wears a crown.

Prepare a presentation of the soliloquy using suggestions a–g on page 77 to help you.

Character

USE WITH ONE OF PAGES 86 TO 94

Shakespeare creates characters in three major ways:

- Their actions: Macbeth murders Duncan; Juliet kills herself for love.
- By what is said about them: Lady Macbeth is called 'fiend-like'; Iago is often called 'honest' – but he's not!
- Through their own language: Iago's own words reveal what he is really like.

Every character has his or her distinctive voice. Tybalt in *Romeo and Juliet* speaks only 36 lines in the play, but almost every line expresses his violent, aggressive personality – 'Turn thee, Benvolio, look upon thy death'. King Lear is a much more complex character, but his language is unmistakably his own, full of commands, assertions, questions, and oaths.

Most Shakespeare characters have different sides to their personality. They can behave differently in different situations, and can change over the course of the play. Here are just a few of the aspects of Hamlet.

noble prince

revenger

unhappy adolescent

philosopher

madman

Use the accompanying worksheet. To help your exploration of character, first speak the words aloud. It will give you an initial impression of what the character is like. Then imagine yourself as that character. To find what you are like, ask the following questions:

a Meaning: what am I saying? what thoughts am I expressing?

b Mood: what am I feeling?

c Motivation: what do I want? (why am I saying this?)

d Method: how do I speak? (remember, any speech can be delivered in very different ways)

As you answer these questions, look out for particular features of the language; the vocabulary (are there key words, repetitions?); the imagery, rhythm and syntax (the way the sentences are constructed: smoothly or disjointedly).

As a result of your investigations, stage a presentation of the lines that intensifies dramatic effect.

Character: Juliet's Nurse

USE WITH PAGE 85

In *Romeo and Juliet*, the Nurse recalls an incident in Juliet's childhood:

Lammas-eve
31 July

laid wormwood to my dug
rubbed bitter-tasting plant on her nipple (to wean Juliet)

Shake!
look lively! (shake a leg!)

I trow
I'm sure

th'rood
Christ's cross

holidam
holy dame (Virgin Mary)

stinted
stopped

Even or odd, of all days in the year,
Come Lammas-eve at night shall she be fourteen.
Susan and she – God rest all Christian souls! –
Were of an age. Well, Susan is with God,
She was too good for me. But as I said,
On Lammas-eve at night shall she be fourteen,
That shall she, marry, I remember it well.
'Tis since the earthquake now aleven years,
And she was weaned – I never shall forget it –
Of all the days of the year, upon that day;
For I had then laid wormwood to my dug,
Sitting in the sun under the dove-house wall.
My lord and you were then at Mantua –
Nay, I do bear a brain – but as I said,
When it did taste the wormwood on the nipple
Of my dug, and felt it bitter, pretty fool,
To see it tetchy and fall out wi'th'dug!
'Shake!' quoth the dove-house; 'twas no need, I trow,
To bid me trudge.
And since that time it is aleven years,
For then she could stand high-lone; nay, by th'rood,
She could have run and waddled all about;
For even the day before, she broke her brow,
And then my husband – God be with his soul,
'A was a merry man – took up the child.
'Yea', quoth he, 'dost thou fall upon thy face?
Thou wilt fall backward when thou hast more wit,
Wilt thou not, Jule?' And by my holidam,
The pretty wretch left crying, and said 'Ay'.
To see now how a jest shall come about!
I warrant, and I should live a thousand years,
I never should forget it: 'Wilt thou not, Jule?' quoth he,
And, pretty fool, it stinted, and said 'Ay'.

1 Use with questions a–d on page 85. Step into character as the Nurse and speak her story. On the evidence of her language, suggest what kind of person you think she is.

2 Imagine you are Lady Capulet, Juliet's mother, and the Nurse's employer. Write a character reference for the Nurse.

Character: inside Hamlet's mind

USE WITH PAGE 85

Hamlet's first soliloquy reveals his deepest thoughts. He longs for death but knows that suicide is forbidden by God. He expresses disgust that his mother has remarried so soon after his father's death.

Everlasting God

canon law

Hyperion the sun-god

satyr lecherous creature, half man, half goat

beteem permit

Niobe Queen of Thebes who wept for her dead children

wants lacks

Hercules mythical Greek hero, enormously strong

gallèd sore from weeping

post hurry

O that this too too solid flesh would melt,
Thaw and resolve itself into a dew,
Or that the Everlasting had not fixed
His canon 'gainst self-slaughter. O God, God,
How weary, stale, flat and unprofitable
Seem to me all the uses of this world!
Fie on't, ah fie, 'tis an unweeded garden
That grows to seed, things rank and gross in nature
Possess it merely. That it should come to this!
But two months dead – nay not so much, not two –
So excellent a king, that was to this
Hyperion to a satyr, so loving to my mother
That he might not beteem the winds of heaven
Visit her face too roughly – heaven and earth,
Must I remember? why, she would hang on him
As if increase of appetite had grown
By what it fed on, and yet within a month –
Let me not think on't; frailty, thy name is woman –
A little month, or ere those shoes were old
With which she followed my poor father's body
Like Niobe, all tears, why she, even she –
O God, a beast that wants discourse of reason
Would have mourned longer – married with my uncle,
My father's brother, but no more like my father
Than I to Hercules – within a month,
Ere yet the salt of most unrighteous tears
Had left the flushing in her gallèd eyes,
She married. Oh most wicked speed, to post
With such dexterity to incestuous sheets.
It is not, nor it cannot come to good.
But break, my heart, for I must hold my tongue.

Use with questions a–d on page 85. Hamlet uses a great deal of imagery. Identify as many as you can of the 'pictures' in the lines. Suggest how each one may suggest something about Hamlet's character.

Character: two views of 'honour'

USE WITH PAGE 85

In *King Henry IV part 1,* Hotspur and Falstaff express very different views of honour.

deep
ocean

locks
hair

corrival
equal

HOTSPUR By heaven, methinks it were an easy leap
To pluck bright honour from the pale-faced moon,
Or dive into the bottom of the deep,
Where fathom-line could never touch the ground,
And pluck up drownèd honour by the locks,
So he that doth redeem her thence might wear
Without corrival all her dignities.

The battle of Shrewsbury is about to begin. Prince Hal's words set Falstaff thinking:

pricks
urges

set to
mend

trim reckoning
neat calculation

Detraction
slander

suffer
allow

scutcheon
funeral shield (hung in churches)

catechism
statement of religious belief

FALSTAFF I would 'twere bed-time, Hal, and all well.
HAL Why, thou owest God a death. *Exit*
FALSTAFF 'Tis not due yet – I would be loath to pay him before his day. What need I be so forward with him that calls not on me? Well, 'tis no matter, honour pricks me on. Yea, but how if honour prick me off when I come on, how then? Can honour set to a leg? No. Or an arm? No. Or take away the grief of a wound? No. Honour hath no skill in surgery then? No. What is honour? A word. What is in that word honour? What is that honour? Air. A trim reckoning! Who hath it? He that died a'Wednesday. Doth he feel it? No. Doth he hear it? No. 'Tis insensible, then? Yea, to the dead. But will it not live with the living? No. Why? Detraction will not suffer it. Therefore I'll none of it. Honour is a mere scutcheon – and so ends my catechism. *Exit*

Use with questions a–d on page 85 to help you prepare a dramatic presentation to show the contrasts between the two speakers.

Character: aspects of Caliban

USE WITH PAGE 85

In the list of characters for *The Tempest*, Caliban is called 'a savage and deformed slave'. Other characters call him 'tortoise', 'fish', 'beast', 'monster'. Here are two of Caliban's speeches:

the bigger light/ the less
the sun/moon

charms
spells

sty
imprison me like a pig

This island's mine by Sycorax my mother,
Which thou tak'st from me. When thou cam'st first
Thou strok'st me and made much of me; wouldst give me
Water with berries in't, and teach me how
To name the bigger light, and how the less,
That burn by day and night. And then I loved thee
And showed thee all the qualities o'th'isle,
The fresh springs, brine-pits, barren place and fertile –
Cursèd be I that did so! All the charms
Of Sycorax – toads, beetles, bats – light on you!
For I am all the subjects that you have,
Which first was mine own king; and here you sty me
In this hard rock, whiles you do keep from me
The rest o'th'island.

Be not afeared, the isle is full of noises,
Sounds, and sweet airs, that give delight and hurt not.
Sometimes a thousand twangling instruments
Will hum about mine ears; and sometime voices,
That if I then had waked after long sleep,
Will make me sleep again; and then in dreaming,
The clouds methought would open, and show riches
Ready to drop upon me, that when I waked
I cried to dream again.

1 Use with questions a–d on page 85. Experiment with ways of speaking and staging Caliban's lines, acting out everything he describes.

2 Does Caliban's language match the descriptions of him given at the top of this page? Give reasons for your answer.

Character: aspects of Othello

USE WITH PAGE 85

In the first speech, Othello tells Desdemona, his wife, of the handkerchief she has lost. In the second speech, a little later, he is maddened by jealous thoughts of her unfaithfulness.

charmer witch
amiable beloved
fancies lovers
perdition damnation

That handkerchief
Did an Egyptian to my mother give:
She was a charmer and could almost read
The thoughts of people. She told her, while she kept it,
'Twould make her amiable and subdue my father
Entirely to her love; but if she lost it
Or made a gift of it, my father's eye
Should hold her loathèd and his spirits should hunt
After new fancies. She dying gave it me,
And bid me when my fate would have me wive,
To give it her. I did so, and take heed on't:
Make it a darling, like your precious eye.
To lose't or give't away were such perdition
As nothing else could match.

belie slander
Zounds by God's wounds
fulsome revolting
shadowing overwhelming
instruction reason

Lie with her? Lie on her? We say lie on her when they belie her. Lie with her! Zounds, that's fulsome! Handkerchief – confessions – handkerchief! To confess and be hanged for his labour. First to be hanged and then to confess. I tremble at it. Nature would not invest herself in such shadowing passion without some instruction. It is not words that shakes me thus. Pish! Noses, ears, and lips. Isn't possible? – Confess? Handkerchief? O devil!

He falls in a trance

Use with questions a–d on page 85 to help you deduce as much as you can about Othello's personality, and to stage the two extracts.

Character: Mistress Quickly

USE WITH PAGE 85

In *King Henry IV part 2* Mistress Quickly, Hostess of the tavern, reminds Falstaff of his promises.

parcel-gilt
partly gilded

Dolphin chamber
(name of the inn room)

Wheeson
Whitsun

liking
comparing

singing man
royal chorister

gossip
neighbour

mess
drop

green
unhealed

ere long
soon

thy book-oath
swear on the Bible

FALSTAFF What is the gross sum that I owe thee?

HOSTESS Marry, if thou wert an honest man, thyself and the money too: thou didst swear to me upon a parcel-gilt goblet, sitting in my Dolphin chamber at the round table by a sea-coal fire, upon Wednesday in Wheeson week, when the prince broke thy head for liking his father to a singing man of Windsor – thou didst swear to me then, as I was washing thy wound, to marry me, and make me my lady thy wife. Canst thou deny it? Did not goodwife Keech the butcher's wife come in then and call me gossip Quickly, coming in to borrow a mess of vinegar, telling us she had a good dish of prawns, whereby thou didst desire to eat some, whereby I told thee they were ill for a green wound? And didst thou not, when she was gone downstairs, desire me to be no more so familiarity with such poor people, saying that ere long they should call me madam? And didst thou not kiss me, and bid me fetch thee thirty shillings? I put thee now to thy book-oath, deny it if thou canst.

1. Use with questions a–d on page 85. Try performing the lines both with and without movements and gestures. How would *your* Mistress Quickly speak and act?
2. Mistress Quickly's language is filled with very detailed lists giving particulars of time and place and incidents. Improvise a speech of similar length where she gives further reminders to Falstaff of his promise to marry her.

Character: a villain's thoughts

USE WITH PAGE 85

Richard III begins with a revealing soliloquy by Richard, who is not yet king, but is determined to become so.

Now is the winter of our discontent
Made glorious summer by this sun of York,
And all the clouds that loured upon our house
In the deep bosom of the ocean buried.
Now are our brows bound with victorious wreaths,
Our bruisèd arms hung up for monuments,
Our stern alarums changed to merry meetings,
Our dreadful marches to delightful measures.
Grim-visaged war hath smoothed his wrinkled front,
And now, instead of mounting barbèd steeds
To fright the souls of fearful adversaries,
He capers nimbly in a lady's chamber
To the lascivious pleasing of a lute.
But I, that am not shaped for sportive tricks
Nor made to court an amorous looking-glass;
I, that am rudely stamped, and want love's majesty
To strut before a wanton ambling nymph;
I, that am curtailed of this fair proportion,
Cheated of feature by dissembling Nature,
Deformed, unfinished, sent before my time
Into this breathing world, scarce half made up,
And that so lamely and unfashionable
That dogs bark at me as I halt by them –
Why I, in this weak piping time of peace,
Have no delight to pass away the time,
Unless to spy my shadow in the sun
And descant on mine own deformity.
And therefore, since I cannot prove a lover
To entertain these fair well-spoken days,
I am determined to prove a villain
And hate the idle pleasures of these days.

York
King Edward IV (Richard's brother)

loured upon our house
threatened our family

bruisèd arms
broken weapons

monuments
memorials

alarums
warfare

measures
dances

wrinkled front
frowning forehead

barbèd
armoured

capers
dances foolishly

rudely stamped
rough in appearance

want love's majesty
lack beauty

nymph
pretty woman

curtailed
cut short

descant on
describe

Use with questions a–d on page 85. Is Richard's tone neutral and objective, resentful and bitter, or …? Which words in each line might you speak ironically or contemptuously?

Character: two views of Hamlet

USE WITH PAGE 85

Hamlet reviles Ophelia, whom he once hoped to marry. She sorrows over his fall from nobility to madness.

dowry
wedding gift

calumny
malicious lies

paintings
make-up

jig
dance

make your wantonness your ignorance
pretend your immorality comes from innocence

no mo
no more

expectancy and rose
hope and crowning glory

glass
mirror

mould of form
model of behaviour and taste

Th'observed of all observers
ideal example

blown
blossoming-ripe

Blasted with ecstasy
ruined by madness

HAMLET If thou dost marry, I'll give thee this plague for thy dowry: be thou as chaste as ice, as pure as snow, thou shalt not escape calumny. Get thee to a nunnery, go. Farewell. Or if thou wilt needs marry, marry a fool, for wise men know well enough what monsters you make of them. To a nunnery go, and quickly too. Farewell.

OPHELIA O heavenly powers, restore him!

HAMLET I have heard of your paintings too, well enough. God hath given you one face and you make yourselves another. You jig, you amble, and you lisp, you nickname God's creatures, and make your wantonness your ignorance. Go to, I'll no more on't, it hath made me mad. I say we will have no mo marriages. Those that are married already, all but one shall live, the rest shall keep as they are. To a nunnery, go.

Exit

OPHELIA Oh what a noble mind is here o'erthrown!
The courtier's, soldier's, scholar's, eye, tongue, sword,
Th'expectancy and rose of the fair state,
The glass of fashion and the mould of form,
Th'observed of all observers, quite, quite down,
And I of ladies most deject and wretched,
That sucked the honey of his music vows,
Now see that noble and most sovereign reason,
Like sweet bells jangled, out of time and harsh;
That unmatched form and feature of blown youth
Blasted with ecstasy. Oh woe is me
T'have seen what I have seen, see what I see.

1 Work in pairs. Take parts as Hamlet and Ophelia and use with questions a–d on page 85.

2 Show the contrast between what Hamlet says and how Ophelia describes him. For example, you might 'intercut' the speeches: Ophelia speaks a line, then Hamlet speaks a short section and so on. Use appropriate tones for both speakers.

Character: Cassius described

USE WITH PAGE 85

In *Julius Caesar*, Caesar reveals what he thinks of Cassius.

CAESAR Let me have men about me that are fat,
Sleek-headed men and such as sleep a-nights.
Yond Cassius has a lean and hungry look,
He thinks too much: such men are dangerous.
ANTONY Fear him not, Caesar, he's not dangerous,
He is a noble Roman and well given.
CAESAR Would he were fatter! But I fear him not.
Yet if my name were liable to fear
I do not know the man I should avoid
So soon as that spare Cassius. He reads much,
He is a great observer, and he looks
Quite through the deeds of men. He loves no plays,
As thou dost, Antony, he hears no music;
Seldom he smiles, and smiles in such a sort
As if he mocked himself and scorned his spirit
That could be moved to smile at any thing.
Such men as he be never at heart's ease
Whiles they behold a greater than themselves,
And therefore are they very dangerous.
I rather tell thee what is to be feared
Than what I fear: for always I am Caesar.
Come on my right hand, for this ear is deaf,
And tell me truly what thou think'st of him.

well given friendly

1 Use with questions a–d on page 85. What can you deduce about Caesar's character from what he says about Cassius?

2 Caesar does not use imagery. Select each description of Cassius and add a simile of your own: 'lean and hungry look, like a ...'; 'He thinks too much, like a ...' . Use your images to present a portrait of Cassius, either as a short play or as a drawing.

3 Imagine you are Cassius. Use Caesar's language as a model to write *your* view of Caesar.

Creating atmosphere

USE WITH ONE OF PAGES 96 TO 104

Shakespeare's theatre did not have the sophisticated technology that today creates elaborate sets in modern theatres. His scene painting was done in words, his lighting effects achieved through language. Shakespeare's basic resources were the human voice, the human body and the bare stage of the Globe Theatre. Elizabethan audiences went to 'hear' a play. Today's audiences go to 'see' a film or play.

Shakespeare knew that he must create atmosphere and setting through language. When *King Henry V* was first staged, the play was performed with a minimum of props or scenery. In the Prologue, Chorus acknowledges the impossibility of representing great battles between the warring armies of England and France with only a few actors on a bare stage. The audience's imagination must respond to the language of the play, creating in their minds battles between France and England:

> Think when we talk of horses that you see them
> Printing their proud hooves i'th'receiving earth.

In Shakespeare's theatre the atmosphere of any play was created through words. Language produced the dramatic effect of fear or joy, day or night, forest or tempest-racked sea, graveyards or open heath, battlefields or castle battlements:

> 'Tis now the very witching time of night,
> When churchyards yawn, and hell itself breathes out
> Contagion to this world.

> Blow, winds, and crack your cheeks! Rage, blow,
> You cataracts and hurricanoes spout ...
> Rumble thy bellyful; spit, fire; spout, rain!

> Shall I not then be stifled in the vault,
> To whose foul mouth no healthsome air breathes in

In the extract on the accompanying worksheet, Shakespeare creates atmosphere through language.

a Read the extract aloud to gain a first impression.

b Identify the ways in which atmosphere is built up through imagery, lists, vocabulary, repetitions, antithesis, etc. Explore different ways of speaking the lines.

c Use your findings to stage a dramatic presentation of the extract to convey an intense feeling of time, place or emotional climate. This could be done through acting out, choral speaking, accompanying actions, rituals, etc.

Creating atmosphere: imagine!

USE WITH PAGE 95

At the opening of *King Henry V*, Chorus acknowledges that the audience's imagination must respond to the language of the play, creating in their minds the battles between France and England.

muse
goddess of poetry

Assume the port of
appear like

scaffold
stage

cockpit
theatre

casques
helmets

since a crooked ... million
just as the tiny addition of '0's can turn 10 into 1,000,000, so few actors ('ciphers') can portray thousands

Piece out
remedy, make perfect

puissance
armies

O for a muse of fire, that would ascend
The brightest heaven of invention,
A kingdom for a stage, princes to act,
And monarchs to behold the swelling scene.
Then should the warlike Harry, like himself,
Assume the port of Mars, and at his heels
(Leashed in, like hounds) should famine, sword and fire
Crouch for employment. But pardon, gentles all,
The flat unraisèd spirits, that hath dared,
On this unworthy scaffold, to bring forth
So great an object. Can this cockpit hold
The vasty fields of France? Or may we cram
Within this wooden O the very casques
That did affright the air at Agincourt?
Oh, pardon: since a crooked figure may
Attest in little place a million,
And let us, ciphers to this great account,
On your imaginary forces work.
Suppose within the girdle of these walls
Are now confined two mighty monarchies,
Whose high uprearèd and abutting fronts
The perilous narrow ocean parts asunder.
Piece out our imperfections with your thoughts.
Into a thousand parts divide one man,
And make imaginary puissance.
Think when we talk of horses that you see them
Printing their proud hooves i'th'receiving earth,
For 'tis your thoughts that now must deck our kings,
Carry them here and there, jumping o'er times,
Turning th'accomplishment of many years
Into an hour-glass.

Use with suggestions a–c on page 95. To help your preparation, identify the words that suggest great and glorious events, and the sentences in which Chorus apologises for the inadequacies of theatre in portraying realistic battles.

Creating atmosphere: mourning

USE WITH PAGE 95

In *Cymbeline*, two brothers grieve over Imogen whom they believe to be dead.

physic
medicine

Consign
submit

exorciser
person who drives out devils

forbear
spare, avoid

consummation
death, end of life

Fear no more the heat o'th'sun,
    Nor the furious winter's rages,
Thou thy worldly task hath done,
    Home art gone and ta'en thy wages.
Golden lads and girls all must,
As chimney-sweepers, come to dust.

Fear no more the frown o'th'great,
    Thou art past the tyrant's stroke
Care no more to clothe and eat,
    To thee the reed is as the oak.
The sceptre, learning, physic, must
All follow this and come to dust.

Fear no more the lightning-flash,
    Nor th'all-dreaded thunder-stone.
Fear not slander, censure rash,
    Thou hast finish'd joy and moan.
All lovers young, all lovers must
Consign to thee and come to dust.

No exorciser harm thee!
Nor no witchcraft charm thee!
Ghost unlaid forbear thee!
Nothing ill come near thee!
Quiet consummation have,
And renownèd be thy grave!

In *Romeo and Juliet* Capulet mourns for Juliet.

office
proper function

dirge
funeral song

corse
corpse

All things that we ordainèd festival,
Turn from their office to black funeral:
Our instruments to melancholy bells,
Our wedding cheer to a sad burial feast;
Our solemn hymns to sullen dirges change;
Our bridal flowers serve for a buried corse;
And all things change them to the contrary.

1 Use with suggestions a–c on page 95.

2 In the eighteenth and nineteenth centuries, theatre productions often added a scene to show the funeral of Juliet. Work in a large group to stage Juliet's funeral procession, using also the language from *Cymbeline*. Speak, sing or chant the words, and divide up the language in any way that you think appropriate.

Creating atmosphere: fear

USE WITH PAGE 95

It is the night before Juliet's wedding to Paris. But she is already secretly married to Romeo who has been banished from Verona for slaying her cousin, Tybalt. Alone in her bedroom she thinks fearfully of the plan that Friar Lawrence has devised for her to escape the second marriage. If she drinks the 'poison', it will cause her to sleep a sleep like death itself.

conceit
thought

mandrakes
plants that were believed to grow beneath gallows and to shriek as they were pulled up

Environèd
surrounded

spit
pierce, impale

How if, when I am laid into the tomb,
I wake before the time that Romeo
Come to redeem me? There's a fearful point!
Shall I not then be stifled in the vault,
To whose foul mouth no healthsome air breathes in,
And there die strangled ere my Romeo comes?
Or if I live, is it not very like
The horrible conceit of death and night,
Together with the terror of the place –
As in a vault, an ancient receptacle,
Where for this many hundred years the bones
Of all my buried ancestors are packed,
Where bloody Tybalt, yet but green in earth,
Lies fest'ring in his shroud, where, as they say,
At some hours in the night spirits resort –
Alack, alack, is it not like that I,
So early waking – what with loathsome smells,
And shrieks like mandrakes' torn out of the earth,
That living mortals hearing them run mad –
O, if I wake, shall I not be distraught,
Environèd with all these hideous fears,
And madly play with my forefathers' joints,
And pluck the mangled Tybalt from his shroud,
And in this rage, with some great kinsman's bone,
As with a club, dash out my desp'rate brains?
O look! methinks I see my cousin's ghost
Seeking out Romeo that did spit his body
Upon a rapier's point. Stay, Tybalt, stay!
Romeo, Romeo, Romeo! Here's drink – I drink to thee.

[She falls upon her bed, within the curtains.]

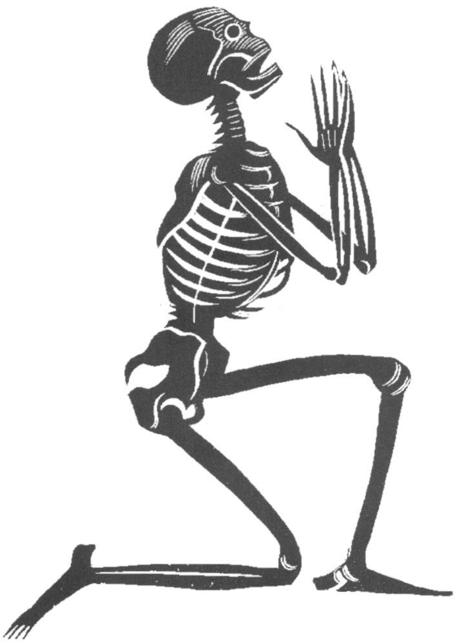

1 Use with suggestions a–c on page 95.

2 In a group, one person reads Juliet's lines, while the others echo every word to do with fear or death. Afterwards talk together about how such words and Juliet's many questions help build up an atmosphere of fear and suspense.

Creating atmosphere: the supernatural

USE WITH PAGE 95

Lady Macbeth is full of murderous thoughts about King Duncan.

compunctious compassionate

fell deadly

gall bitter poison

pall wrap (as in a funeral pall or cloak)

dunnest darkest

The raven himself is hoarse,
That croaks the fatal entrance of Duncan
Under my battlements. Come, you spirits
That tend on mortal thoughts, unsex me here
And fill me from the crown to the toe topfull
Of direst cruelty; make thick my blood,
Stop up th'access and passage to remorse
That no compunctious visitings of nature
Shake my fell purpose nor keep peace between
Th'effect and it. Come to my woman's breasts
And take my milk for gall, you murd'ring ministers,
Wherever in your sightless substances
You wait on nature's mischief. Come, thick night,
And pall thee in the dunnest smoke of hell,
That my keen knife see not the wound it makes,
Nor heaven peep through the blanket of the dark,
To cry, 'Hold, hold.'

Macbeth thinks of the oncoming night in which he will have Banquo murdered.

seeling blinding (hawks' eyes were 'seeled' by sewing them up)

Come, seeling night,
Scarf up the tender eye of pitiful day
And with thy bloody and invisible hand
Cancel and tear to pieces that great bond
Which keeps me pale. Light thickens,
And the crow makes wing to th'rooky wood;
Good things of day begin to droop and drowse,
Whiles night's black agents to their preys do rouse.

1. Use with suggestions a–c on page 95.
2. Experiment with different ways of speaking both speeches as if they were spells: whisper them, hiss then fiercely, speak them as if in a trance. Try emphasising all the words of command: 'Come', 'unsex', 'fill', 'make thick', etc.

Creating atmosphere: Lear's rage

USE WITH PAGE 95

King Lear, maddened by how his daughters have treated him, rages against the storm.

cataracts and hurricanoes
waterfalls and waterspouts

cocks
weathercocks

thought-executing
mind-numbing, swifter than thought

Vaunt-couriers
forerunners

thick rotundity
round-belliedness

germens
seeds

court holy water
flattery

tax
accuse

subscription
loyalty

servile
inferior

high-engendered
sky-born

LEAR Blow, winds, and crack your cheeks! Rage, blow,
You cataracts and hurricanoes, spout
Till you have drenched our steeples, drowned the cocks!
You sulph'rous and thought-executing fires,
Vaunt-couriers of oak-cleaving thunderbolts,
Singe my white head; and thou all-shaking thunder,
Strike flat the thick rotundity o'th'world,
Crack nature's moulds, all germens spill at once
That makes ingrateful man.

FOOL O nuncle, court holy water in a dry house is better than this rain-water out o'door. Good nuncle, in, ask thy daughters blessing. Here's a night pities neither wise men nor fools.

LEAR Rumble thy bellyful; spit, fire; spout, rain!
Nor rain, wind, thunder, fire are my daughters.
I tax not you, you elements, with unkindness.
I never gave you kingdom, called you children.
You owe me no subscription. Then let fall
Your horrible pleasure. Here I stand your slave,
A poor, infirm, weak, and despised old man;
But yet I call you servile ministers,
That will with two pernicious daughters join
Your high-engendered battles 'gainst a head
So old and white as this, O, ho! 'tis foul.

1 Use with suggestions a–c on page 95 to help you stage Lear's lines. If you add sound effects, remember that the audience must hear every word Lear speaks.

2 Do Lear's emotions change from line to line? Find some way of recording the progress and intensity of his feelings as suggested by the language.

3 King Lear's language throughout the play is full of commands. How many commands can you find in the lines? Suggest how Lear's different commands help create the atmosphere of the scene.

Creating atmosphere: confusion

USE WITH PAGE 95

anointed temple
most holy place

Gorgon
Medusa, a mythical woman with snakes for hair; anyone who saw her was turned to stone

counterfeit
imitation

The great doom's image
wall-painting of the Day of Judgement (when the dead rose from their graves)

countenance
confirm, view

Macduff has just discovered the body of the murdered King Duncan.

MACDUFF O horror, horror, horror,
Tongue nor heart cannot conceive, nor name thee.
MACBETH *and* LENNOX What's the matter?
MACDUFF Confusion now hath made his masterpiece:
Most sacrilegious murder hath broke ope
The Lord's anointed temple and stole thence
The life o'th'building.
MACBETH What is't you say, the life?
LENNOX Mean you his majesty?
MACDUFF Approach the chamber and destroy your sight
With a new Gorgon. Do not bid me speak:
See and then speak yourselves.

Exeunt MACBETH *and* LENNOX

Awake, awake!
Ring the alarum bell! Murder and treason!
Banquo and Donaldbain! Malcolm, awake,
Shake off this downy sleep, death's counterfeit,
And look on death itself. Up, up, and see
The great doom's image. Malcolm, Banquo,
As from your graves rise up and walk like sprites
To countenance this horror.

Gorgon's head

1 Use with suggestions a–c on page 95. To help your preparation consider each line and suggest how it adds to the atmosphere created by the discovery of the murdered King.

2 Can Shakespeare's language sometimes be spoken in a different order from that in which it appears in the script? Work in a large group. Everyone walks around the room, greeting others with a line or short section from anywhere in the extract. Don't worry about which character is speaking, just say the lines in any order.

Afterwards, work in small groups to discuss whether the lines could be spoken in a different order – and by different characters – and still be meaningful and dramatically effective.

Creating atmosphere: Dover cliff

USE WITH PAGE 95

In *King Lear*, Edgar deceives his blind father by describing an imaginary view of Dover cliff:

Come on, sir, here's the place. Stand still. How fearful
And dizzy 'tis to cast one's eyes so low.
The crows and choughs that wing the midway air
Show scarce so gross as beetles. Half-way down
Hangs one that gathers samphire, dreadful trade!
Methinks he seems no bigger than his head.
The fishermen that walk upon the beach
Appear like mice, and yon tall anchoring barque
Diminished to her cock; her cock, a buoy
Almost too small for sight. The murmuring surge,
That on th'unnumbered idle pebble chafes,
Cannot be heard so high. I'll look no more,
Lest my brain turn and the deficient sight
Topple down headlong.

choughs
jackdaws

gross
large

samphire
edible plant collected from cliffs

barque
ship

cock
small boat towed behind a larger one

th'unnumbered idle pebble
innumerable shifting pebbles

deficient
fake, imperfect

1 Use with suggestions a–c on page 95.

2 Edgar is not telling the truth. He invents the picture of Dover cliff because his blind father wishes to leap from the cliff edge to end his suffering. Identify the ways in which the language creates a sense of dizzying height: for example, as one person speaks, the others echo every word or phrase that creates the effect of height.

3 Use the line as a model for a piece of your own writing, in prose or verse, that imaginatively describes a particular place. Try using onomatopoeia – words which sound like the thing they describe, as in Edgar's 'The murmuring surge, That on th'unnumbered idle pebble chafes'.

Creating atmosphere: music

USE WITH PAGE 95

In *The Merchant of Venice*, Lorenzo describes the music of the spheres.

How sweet the moonlight sleeps upon this bank!
Here will we sit, and let the sounds of music
Creep in our ears; soft stillness and the night
Become the touches of sweet harmony.
Sit, Jessica. Look how the floor of heaven
Is thick inlaid with patens of bright gold.
There's not the smallest orb which thou behold'st
But in his motion like an angel sings,
Still choiring to the young-eyed cherubins.
Such harmony is in immortal souls,
But whilst this muddy vesture of decay
Doth grossly close it in, we cannot hear it.

bank
grassy slope

Become
fit

Jessica
Lorenzo's wife (Shylock's daughter)

patens
small plates (used at Holy Communion)

orb
star

choiring
singing

cherubins
beautiful angels

muddy vesture of decay
human body

grossly close it in
crudely cover it

The 'heavens' were painted on the roof of the Globe stage. The Elizabethans believed that the planets moved on crystal spheres whose movement created delightful music. Only the gods could hear it, humans could not.

1. Use with suggestions a–c on page 95. To help your preparation, identify how the vocabulary creates the atmosphere: for example, pick out the imagery and words connected with the senses.
2. Write your own description of a landscape or view to be spoken by someone like Lorenzo, newly-married and deeply in love.

Atmosphere: a statue comes to life

USE WITH PAGE 95

Near the end of *The Winter's Tale*, Leontes, King of Sicilia, is shown a statue of his wife Hermione. For sixteen years he has believed that she is dead, killed by his jealousy. Paulina, a friend of Hermione, says she can bring the statue of the dead queen to life.

forbear
withdraw

Quit presently
immediately leave

awake your faith
believe in miracles

start not
don't be afraid

shun
leave, avoid

double
twice (Leontes believes that he has earlier caused Hermione's death)

PAULINA Either forbear,
Quit presently the chapel, or resolve you
For more amazement. If you can behold it,
I'll make the statue move indeed, descend
And take you by the hand. But then you'll think –
Which I protest against – I am assisted
By wicked powers.

LEONTES What you can make her do
I am content to look on, what to speak
I am content to hear; for 'tis as easy
To make her speak as move.

PAULINA It is required
You do awake your faith. Then all stand still;
On: those that think it is unlawful business
I am about, let them depart.

LEONTES Proceed.
No foot shall stir.

PAULINA Music; awake her; strike.

Music

'Tis time; descend; be stone no more; approach;
Strike all that look upon with marvel. Come;
I'll fill your grave up. Stir; nay, come away;
Bequeath to death your numbness, for from him
Dear life redeems you. You perceive she stirs.

Hermione moves, and begins to descend

Start not: her actions shall be holy as
You hear my spell is lawful. [*To Leontes*] Do not shun her
Until you see her die again, for then
You kill her double. Nay, present your hand:
When she was young you wooed her; now, in age,
Is she become the suitor?

LEONTES O, she's warm!

Use suggestions a–c on page 95 to prepare your own staging. Identify all the clues in the language that can help you build up an emotionally charged atmosphere. Leontes believes that Hermione is dead, so how does he behave as she comes to life? Work out how you might act out the stage direction *Hermione moves, and begins to descend* to greatest dramatic effect.

Themes

USE WITH ONE OF PAGES 106 TO 115

Each Shakespeare play has its own particular themes: jealousy in *Othello*, ambition in *Macbeth*, nature and nurture in *The Tempest*, sight and blindness in *King Lear*, and so on. However, four themes are found in every Shakespeare play: conflict, appearance and reality, order and disorder, change.

A Conflict: the strife of rivals in love or war; within families (parents against children, brother versus brother), or between families (Montagues versus Capulets in *Romeo and Juliet*), and so on.

B Appearance and reality: things and people are not what they seem. Women disguise themselves as men; evil intentions are hidden behind masks of friendship; characters pretend to be mad.

C Order and disorder: the disturbance in persons, society and nature. King Lear's sanity is destroyed, his kingdom is divided, nature itself is wracked by storm.

D Change (metamorphosis): in every play characters change in some way. Many learn new understandings from the suffering they endure. Kings and tyrants finally succumb to death. Nick Bottom is magically transformed into an ass in *A Midsummer Night's Dream*.

---

1 Work in a small group. Devise a tableau – a frozen picture or still photograph – to show one of the four themes above. Present your tableau, frozen for one minute, for other groups to guess which theme is being portrayed.

2 Identify how each of the four themes is present in the play you are currently studying.

3 Suggest how each of the four themes is present in today's society.

4 The accompanying worksheet contains an extract that illustrates a theme. Explore ways of making a dramatic presentation of the lines. It will help you to identify the features of the language that give the theme dramatic life: for example, vocabulary, imagery, antitheses, lists, etc.

There are many ways in which each extract can be spoken and presented: consider tone, pauses, emphasis, speed, repetitions, movement, gesture, accompanying sound effects, etc. There is no single 'right' way!

Themes: appearance and reality 1

USE WITH PAGE 105

In *The Merchant of Venice* Bassanio reflects on false appearance in law, religion, war and beauty.

So may the outward shows be least themselves:
The world is still deceived with ornament.
In law, what plea so tainted and corrupt
But, being seasoned with a gracious voice,
Obscures the show of evil? In religion,
What damnèd error but some sober brow
Will bless it and approve it with a text,
Hiding the grossness with fair ornament?
There is no vice so simple but assumes
Some mark of virtue on his outward parts.
How many cowards whose hearts are all as false
As stayers of sand, wear yet upon their chins
The beards of Hercules and frowning Mars,
Who inward searched have livers white as milk,
And these assume but valour's excrement
To render them redoubted. Look on beauty,
And you shall see 'tis purchased by the weight,
Which therein works a miracle in nature,
Making them lightest that wear most of it.
So are those crispèd snaky golden locks
Which maketh such wanton gambols with the wind
Upon supposèd fairness, often known
To be the dowry of a second head,
The skull that bred them in the sepulchre.
Thus ornament is but the guilèd shore
To a most dangerous sea.

seasoned disguised, flavoured

sober brow serious face

text quotation from a holy book

stayers stairs or ropes

Hercules immensely strong hero in Greek mythology

Mars god of war

inward searched when the true nature is revealed

valour's excrement a brave man's beard

redoubted feared

crispèd curled

wanton playful

dowry gift

sepulchre grave

guilèd treacherous

1 Use with Activity 4 on page 105. Bassanio lists how people are different from what they seem. Find an active way of emphasising the rhythm in the contrasts between appearance and reality. For example, you could use your hands as scales, or turn bodily at each contrast.

2 Write four to six lines of your own to add further examples to Bassanio's list of people who are not what they seem.

Themes: appearance and reality 2

USE WITH PAGE 105

King Lear's scathing portrayal of authority condemns high-ranking hypocrites who are not what they seem.

yon justice
yonder judge

rails upon
criticises

handy-dandy
make a guess, both are equal

cur
dog

beadle
parish officer (who punished prostitutes)

in that kind
in the same way

usurer
moneylender

cozener
cheat

pygmy's straw
tiny, weak weapon

able 'em
support them

LEAR What, art mad? A man may see how this world goes with no eyes; look with thine ears. See how yon justice rails upon yon simple thief. Hark in thine ear: change places, and handy-dandy, which is the justice, which is the thief? Thou hast seen a farmer's dog bark at a beggar?

GLOUCESTER Ay, sir.

LEAR And the creature run from the cur? There thou mightst behold the great image of authority. A dog's obeyed in office.
Thou rascal beadle, hold thy bloody hand.
Why dost thou lash that whore? Strip thy own back.
Thou hotly lusts to use her in that kind
For which thou whip'st her. The usurer hangs the cozener.
Through tattered clothes great vices do appear:
Robes and furred gowns hide all. Plate sin with gold,
And the strong lance of justice hurtless breaks;
Arm it in rags, a pygmy's straw does pierce it.
None does offend, none, I say none. I'll able 'em.
Take that of me, my friend, who have the power
To seal th'accuser's lips. Get thee glass eyes,
And, like a scurvy politician, seem
To see the things thou dost not.

1 Use with Activity 4 on page 105 to help you find a dramatically effective way of presenting Lear's lines. This should portray all the contrasts he makes between appearance and reality.

2 Add to Lear's list several more examples of hypocrisy by people with high status.

Themes: appearance and reality 3

USE WITH PAGE 105

In *Twelfth Night*, Viola is disguised as a boy in the service of Duke Orsino. Orsino sends her to tell Olivia of his love. Now Viola (who loves Orsino) fears that Olivia has fallen in love with her.

churlish messenger rude person who has brought the ring (Malvolio)

pregnant enemy crafty fiend, the devil

proper-false handsome deceivers

waxen easily moulded, changeable

fadge turn out, develop

dote on be infatuated with

thriftless unprofitable, wasted

I left no ring with her: what means this lady?
Fortune forbid my outside have not charmed her!
She made good view of me, indeed so much
That, methought, her eyes had lost her tongue,
For she did speak in starts distractedly.
She loves me sure; the cunning of her passion
Invites me in this churlish messenger.
None of my lord's ring? Why, he sent her none;
I am the man; if it be so, as 'tis,
Poor lady, she were better love a dream.
Disguise, I see thou art a wickedness,
Wherein the pregnant enemy does much.
How easy is it for the proper-false
In women's waxen hearts to set their forms!
Alas, our frailty is the cause, not we,
For such as we are made of, such we be.
How will this fadge? My master loves her dearly,
And I (poor monster) fond as much on him
As she (mistaken) seems to dote on me.
What will become of this? As I am man,
My state is desperate for my master's love;
As I am woman – now alas the day! –
What thriftless sighs shall poor Olivia breathe?
O time, thou must untangle this, not I;
It is too hard a knot for me t'untie.

1 Use Activity 4 on page 105 to help you prepare a presentation that highlights the theme of appearance and reality.

2 Viola's soliloquy is rather like a conversation. She asks herself questions and tries to answer them. Work in pairs and speak the soliloquy as a conversation, either face to face or as though on the telephone.

Themes: order and disorder

USE WITH PAGE 105

In *Troilus and Cressida*, Ulysses expounds the ideology of degree: the belief that nature and society have a proper, hierarchical order. If that order is disturbed, chaos results. Just as disruption of the planets causes earthquakes and other catastrophes in nature, so the overthrow of hierarchy in society causes anarchy in every social institution.

portents
evil omens

deracinate
uproot

degree
hierarchical authority

from dividable shores
between nations

primogenitive and due of birth
rights of inheritance

Prerogative
privilege

But when the planets
In evil mixture to disorder wander,
What plagues and what portents, what mutiny,
What raging of the sea, shaking of earth,
Commotion in the winds, frights, changes, horrors,
Divert and crack, rend and deracinate
The unity and married calm of states
Quite from their fixure! O, when degree is shaked,
Which is the ladder to all high designs,
The enterprise is sick. How could communities,
Degrees in schools, and brotherhoods in cities,
Peaceful commerce from dividable shores,
The primogenitive and due of birth,
Prerogative of age, crowns, sceptres, laurels,
But by degree, stand in authentic place?
Take but degree away, untune that string,
And hark what discord follows!

'untune that string'. The final two lines use a metaphor from music: just as untuning a violin string causes musical disharmony, so the overthrow of hierarchy in society causes social disharmony and strife.

1 Use with Activity 4 on page 105. Begin by speaking the lines in three ways: as if you believed them to be utterly true; then, as if you believed them to be utterly false; then as if you only half believed them.

2 Find ways of portraying the various lists in the lines – and how each item changes when hierarchy is overturned.

2 What is your own view of 'degree'? Organise a class debate on whether you agree with Ulysses' argument: for example, as expressed in the final two lines.

Themes: conflict

USE WITH PAGE 105

In *Henry VI part 3*, King Henry reflects that the battle of Towton is like the conflicts in nature between day and night, sea and wind.

fares
progresses

contend
fight

equal poise
even balance

fell
cruel

This battle fares like to the morning's war,
When dying clouds contend with growing light,
What time the shepherd, blowing of his nails,
Can neither call it perfect day nor night.
Now sways it this way, like a mighty sea
Forced by the tide to combat with the wind;
Now sways it that way, like the self-same sea
Forced to retire by fury of the wind.
Sometime the flood prevails, and then the wind;
Now one the better, then another best;
Both tugging to be victors, breast to breast,
Yet neither conqueror nor conquerèd;
So is the equal poise of this fell war.

1 Use Activity 4 on page 105 to help you make a dramatic presentation of the lines.

2 Brainstorm a list of other images that might illustrate the theme of conflict. Select two or three items from your list and make up a few lines for each in the same style as those above.

Themes: change – death

USE WITH PAGE 105

In the graveyard, the gravedigger (Clown) hands Hamlet the skull of Yorick, the king's jester.

lien you
lain, been buried

Rhenish
Rhine wine

of most excellent fancy
with a wonderful sense of humour

gibes
jokes

were wont ... roar
make everyone at dinner laugh uproariously

chop-fallen
miserable (down in the mouth)

paint
put on make-up

favour
appearance

CLOWN Here's a skull now: this skull hath lien you i'th'earth three and twenty years.

HAMLET Whose was it?

CLOWN A whoreson mad fellow's it was. Whose do you think it was?

HAMLET Nay I know not.

CLOWN A pestilence on him for a mad rogue, a poured a flagon of Rhenish on my head once. This same skull sir, was Yorick's skull, the king's jester.

HAMLET This?

CLOWN E'en that.

HAMLET Let me see. [*Takes the skull.*] Alas poor Yorick! I knew him Horatio, a fellow of infinite jest, of most excellent fancy, he hath borne me on his back a thousand times – and now how abhorred in my imagination it is! My gorge rises at it. Here hung those lips that I have kissed I know not how oft. Where be your gibes now? your gambols, your songs, your flashes of merriment that were wont to set the table on a roar? Not one now, to mock your own grinning? Quite chop-fallen? Now get you to my lady's chamber, and tell her, let her paint an inch thick, to this favour she must come. Make her laugh at that.

Hamlet contrasts the Yorick he knew with what Yorick has now become. Use with Activity 4 on page 105 and find a dramatic way of presenting the lines to bring out as powerfully as you can the theme of change by death.

Themes: change – love

USE WITH PAGE 105

In *The Two Gentlemen of Verona*, Speed tells how his master Valentine has been transformed by love.

VALENTINE Why, how know you that I am in love?

SPEED Marry, by these special marks: first, you have learned, like Sir Proteus, to wreathe your arms like a malcontent; to relish a love-song like a robin redbreast; to walk alone like one that had the pestilence; to sigh like a schoolboy that had lost his ABC; to weep like a young wench that had buried her grandam; to fast like one that takes diet; to watch like one that fears robbing; to speak puling like a beggar at Hallowmas. You were wont, when you laughed, to crow like a cock; when you walked, to walk like one of the lions; when you fasted, it was presently after dinner; when you looked sadly, it was for want of money. And now you are metamorphised with a mistress, that, when I look on you, I can hardly think you my master.

Marry
by Saint Mary (a mild oath)

Sir Proteus
Valentine's friend

pestilence
plague

ABC
(schoolbooks)

grandam
grandmother

watch
stay awake

puling ... Hallowmas
whine like a pauper begging for money on All Saints Day (November 1)

wont
accustomed

cock
cockerel

presently
immediately

metamorphised
changed

'Wreathe your arms like a malcontent': twist your arms together like a melancholy lover.

1 Use with Activity 4 on page 105 to help you devise a presentation of the lines called 'Before love – and after!' As one person narrates, the others act out what is described. Change the order of the lines if you wish.

2 Write and act out a modern equivalent. How does someone change their behaviour today because of falling in love?

Themes: what is the play about?

USE WITH PAGE 105

There is no single answer to the question 'What is this Shakespeare play about?' None of his plays can be adequately summed up in a few words. But every play has a number of distinctive themes. These include, for example: justice, nature, sight and blindness in *King Lear*, revenge, madness and delay in *Hamlet*, how family feuds destroy love in *Romeo and Juliet*, and so on.

The language of every play also has its own distinctive qualities, which reflect in some way the themes and nature of that play. For example, *King Lear*, so much concerned with the nature of authority, is filled with the language of imperious authority: commands, assertions, exclamations and vehement curses.

In *Measure for Measure*, the corrupt judge, Angelo, desires to seduce Isabella. He offers to spare her brother Claudio's life in exchange for her virginity. This illustration of the cover expresses one of the play's central themes: justice.

Justice weighs alternative claims to right and truth. Throughout the play the frequent use of antithesis (words that are balanced opposites) mirrors that 'weighing' process. On every page of the play a character compares or weighs one person or thing against another, as in the Duke's judgement that promises to balance punishment with crime:

> An Angelo for Claudio, death for death;
> Haste still plays haste, and leisure answers leisure;
> Like doth quit like, and measure still for measure

Design a cover for a Shakespeare play of your choice. Your cover should symbolise what you think is important about the language and themes of the play.

Themes: fathers and daughters

USE WITH PAGE 105

Lord Capulet wishes his daughter Juliet to marry Paris, and is enraged by Juliet's refusal.

wrought
obtained, persuaded

chopt-logic
riddles

minion
spoilt brat

fettle your fine joints
get ready
(the expression comes from grooming a horse)

'gainst
against, in preparation for

hurdle
frame on which prisoners were dragged to execution

tallow
pale, waxy

hilding
useless person

CAPULET How now, wife,
Have you delivered to her our decree?
LADY CAPULET Ay, sir, but she will none, she gives you thanks.
I would the fool were married to her grave.
CAPULET Soft, take me with you, take me with you, wife.
How, will she none? doth she not give us thanks?
Is she not proud? doth she not count her blest,
Unworthy as she is, that we have wrought
So worthy a gentleman to be her bride?
JULIET Not proud you have, but thankful that you have:
Proud can I never be of what I hate,
But thankful even for hate that is meant love.
CAPULET How how, how how, chopt-logic? What is this?
'Proud', and 'I thank you', and 'I thank you not',
And yet 'not proud', mistress minion you?
Thank me no thankings, nor proud me no prouds,
But fettle your fine joints 'gainst Thursday next,
To go with Paris to Saint Peter's Church,
Or I will drag thee on a hurdle thither.
Out, you green-sickness carrion! out, you baggage!
You tallow-face!
LADY CAPULET Fie, fie, what, are you mad?
JULIET Good father, I beseech you on my knees,
Hear me with patience but to speak a word.

[She kneels down]

CAPULET Hang thee, young baggage, disobedient wretch!
I tell thee what: get thee to church a'Thursday,
Or never after look me in the face.
Speak not, reply not, do not answer me!
My fingers itch. Wife, we scarce thought us blest
That God had lent us but this only child,
But now I see this one is one too much,
And that we have a curse in having her
Out on her, hilding!

1 Use with Activity 4 on page 105 to help you prepare a presentation of the lines.

2 Shakespeare himself had two daughters, and it seems likely that he strongly disapproved of the man who married his youngest daughter, Judith. Improvise a meeting between Shakespeare and his daughter in which Judith tells her father that she wishes to marry Thomas Quiney.

Themes: all the world's a stage

USE WITH PAGE 105

In *As You Like It* Jaques sees the world as a stage on which each human life is played out, just as actors play out their own brief scenes.

mewling and puking
crying and vomiting

pard
leopard

bubble reputation
short-lived honour

capon
chicken

saws and modern instances
sayings and boring illustrations

hose
stockings, breeches

shank
leg

sans
without

All the world's a stage,
And all the men and women merely players;
They have their exits and their entrances,
And one man in his time plays many parts,
His Acts being seven ages. At first the infant,
Mewling and puking in the nurse's arms;
Then, the whining schoolboy, with his satchel
And shining morning face, creeping like snail
Unwillingly to school; and then the lover,
Sighing like furnace, with a woeful ballad
Made to his mistress' eyebrow; then, a soldier,
Full of strange oaths, and bearded like the pard,
Jealous in honour, sudden and quick in quarrel,
Seeking the bubble reputation
Even in the cannon's mouth; and then, the justice,
In fair round belly, with good capon lined,
With eyes severe, and beard of formal cut,
Full of wise saws and modern instances,
And so he plays his part; the sixth age shifts
Into the lean and slippered pantaloon,
With spectacles on nose and pouch on side,
His youthful hose, well saved, a world too wide
For his shrunk shank, and his big manly voice,
Turning again toward childish treble, pipes
And whistles in his sound. Last scene of all,
That ends this strange eventful history,
Is second childishness, and mere oblivion,
Sans teeth, sans eyes, sans taste, sans everything.

1. Use with Activity 4 on page 105 to help you work out a presentation of the lines to show the seven ages of man.
2. Write your own version of either 'the seven ages of woman', or 'the seven ages of students'. Act out your script.

Stories

USE WITH ONE OF PAGES 117 TO 122

In each of Shakespeare's plays you can find all kinds of stories. Each of these 'stories within a play' invites you to recreate the story in your mind – or to act it out in your classroom.

In *Macbeth*, for example, the first Act includes the following stories: the wounded Captain's account of Macbeth's feats in battle; Ross's completion of that story, telling of victory; the First Witch's story of the Master of the Tiger; the report of the execution of the Thane of Cawdor; and Macbeth's letter to his wife, giving his version of the story so far.

Such stories have many functions. They help create character, atmosphere and context. They fill gaps and move the play's action along.

Some stories tell of events that happened before the play opens – for example, early in *Hamlet*, Horatio explains why Denmark is arming for war. Others relate events that happen off stage, or give glimpses of characters who never appear but whose actions and personalities help to create the imaginative world of the play – for example, Sycorax, the mother of Caliban in *The Tempest*.

Other stories recapitulate the events of the play. Near the end of the play, Friar Lawrence gives his own version of why Romeo and Juliet died. In the final scene of *Hamlet*, Horatio gives a brief summary of the story he will tell of Hamlet's life. Lady Macbeth, as she sleepwalks, recapitulates her past experience in a nightmare stream of consciousness.

1. Identify the stories told within the play you are currently studying. Select one, pick out its separate elements, and act out each event.

2. On stage, most of these 'stories within the play' are usually only spoken, not acted out. But they offer exciting, active opportunities for groups of students to perform each event as one or more persons narrate.

   Use the accompanying worksheet and identify each separate event in the story. Work out the style, tone and mood in which the story could be told. Experiment with words or phrases you might emphasise or echo for heightened effect. Act out the story as fully as you can: every tiny incident, every small section of language, offers rich opportunities for imaginative dramatisation.

The story of the shipwreck

USE WITH PAGE 116

In *The Tempest*, the spirit Ariel gives Prospero an account of the shipwreck he has brought about.

to point
in exact detail

precursors
forerunners

Neptune
king of the sea

coil
turmoil, confusion

tricks of desperation
despairing actions

PROSPERO Hast thou, spirit, performed to point the tempest
That I bade thee?
ARIEL To every article.
I boarded the king's ship. Now on the beak,
Now in the waist, the deck, in every cabin,
I flamed amazement. Sometime I'd divide
And burn in many places; on the topmast,
The yards and bowsprit, would I flame distinctly,
Then meet and join. Jove's lightning, the precursors
O'th'dreadful thunder-claps, more momentary
And sight-outrunning were not; the fire and cracks
Of sulphurous roaring the most mighty Neptune
Seem to besiege, and make his bold waves tremble,
Yea, his dread trident shake.
PROSPERO My brave spirit!
Who was so firm, so constant, that this coil
Would not infect his reason?
ARIEL Not a soul
But felt a fever of the mad, and played
Some tricks of desperation. All but mariners
Plunged in the foaming brine and quit the vessel,
Then all a-fire with me; the king's son Ferdinand,
With hair up-staring – then like reeds, not hair –
Was the first man that leaped; cried 'Hell is empty,
And all the devils are here.'

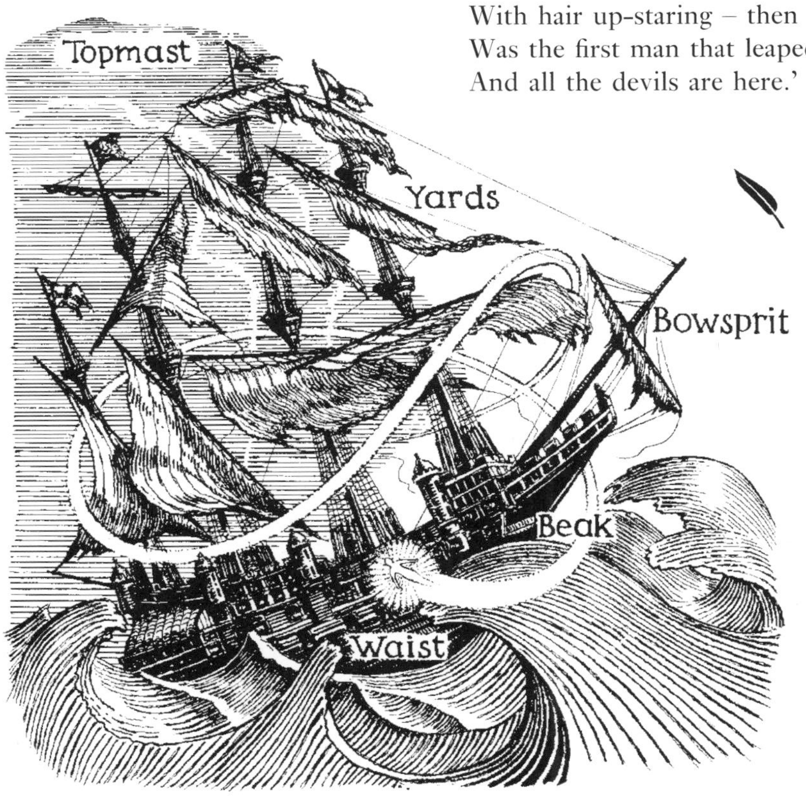

1 As Ariel, 'an airy spirit', tell the story in different ways. Some suggestions might be: whisper it, speak it fearfully, gleefully, breathlessly, urgently, excitedly, mischievously, etc.

2 Use with Activity 2 on page 116 to help you prepare a staging or choral reading of the story. Work in a group, and begin by dividing Ariel's story into sections, so that each small section makes sense. For example, you may choose to make five units of 'Now on the beak' 'Now in the waist' 'the deck' 'in every cabin' 'I flamed amazement', or you may decide to keep the lines together as one unit.

The Ghost's story

USE WITH PAGE 116

Hamlet's father, returning after death as a ghost, recounts how he was murdered by his brother.

secure hour
safe time for relaxation

cursèd hebenon
poison

leperous distilment
evil mixture causing leprosy

posset
clot, thicken

tetter
skin disease

lazar-like
like leprosy

blossom
full bloom

Sleeping within my orchard,
My custom always of the afternoon,
Upon my secure hour thy uncle stole,
With juice of cursèd hebenon in a vial,
And in the porches of my ears did pour
The leperous distilment, whose effect
Holds such an enmity with blood of man
That swift as quicksilver it courses through
The natural gates and alleys of the body,
And with a sudden vigour it doth posset
And curd, like eager droppings into milk,
The thin and wholesome blood. So did it mine,
And a most instant tetter barked about,
Most lazar-like, with vile and loathsome crust,
All my smooth body.
Thus was I, sleeping, by a brother's hand,
Of life, of crown, of queen, at once dispatched;
Cut off even in the blossoms of my sin,
Unhouseled, disappointed, unaneled;
No reckoning made, but sent to my account
With all my imperfections on my head –
Oh horrible, oh horrible, most horrible!

1 Use with Activity 2 on page 116 to help you prepare a presentation of the Ghost's story, to convey the sense of outraged horror felt by an innocent man, murdered by his own brother.

2 The Ghost's horror springs partly from his religious belief. He was killed 'even in the blossoms of my sin', the image of his sins in full flower. He had no time to confess or redeem his sins ('No reckoning made ...', the image of an unpaid bill). In your preparation, give thought to how to speak 'Unhouseled, disappointed, unaneled' to bring out the religious significance of the three words:

'unhouseled'	without sacrament (the bread and wine of Holy Communion)
'disappointed'	unprepared for death (by confession and absolution)
'unaneled'	unanointed (blessed by being anointed with oil)

Story: nightmare memories

USE WITH PAGE 116

As she sleepwalks, Lady Macbeth's tortured imagination recalls past events in the play.

Yet here's a spot.

Out damned spot! Out, I say! One, two. Why then 'tis time to do't. Hell is murky. Fie, my lord, fie, a soldier, and afeard? What need we fear? Who knows it, when none can call our power to account? Yet who would have thought the old man to have had so much blood in him?

The Thane of Fife Macduff (whose wife was murdered on Macbeth's orders)

mar all with this starting spoil everything with your nervousness

The Thane of Fife had a wife. Where is she now? What, will these hands ne'er be clean? No more o'that, my lord, no more o'that. You mar all with this starting.

Here's the smell of the blood still; all the perfumes of Arabia will not sweeten this little hand. O, O, O.

Wash your hands, put on your night-gown, look not so pale. I tell you yet again. Banquo's buried; he cannot come out on's grave.

To bed, to bed; there's knocking at the gate. Come, come, come, come, give me your hand; what's done cannot be undone. To bed, to bed, to bed.

Exit

Use with Activity 2 on page 116 to help you prepare a dramatic presentation of the lines to heighten the nightmare effect of the language.

If you have studied *Macbeth*, you might add to your presentation earlier lines from the play that Lady Macbeth may be recalling each time she speaks.

Story: Clarence's dream

USE WITH PAGE 116

In *King Richard III*, Clarence reports his dream of drowning.

Methoughts that I had broken from the Tower
And was embarked to cross to Burgundy,
And in my company my brother Gloucester,
Who from my cabin tempted me to walk
Upon the hatches; thence we looked toward England
And cited up a thousand heavy times,
During the wars of York and Lancaster,
That had befallen us. As we paced along
Upon the giddy footing of the hatches,
Methought that Gloucester stumbled, and in falling
Struck me, that thought to stay him, overboard
Into the tumbling billows of the main.
O Lord! Methought what pain it was to drown!
What dreadful noise of waters in mine ears!
What sights of ugly death within mine eyes!
Methoughts I saw a thousand fearful wracks;
A thousand men that fishes gnawed upon;
Wedges of gold, great anchors, heaps of pearl,
Inestimable stones, unvalued jewels,
All scattered in the bottom of the sea.
Some lay in dead men's skulls, and in the holes
Where eyes did once inhabit, there were crept,
As 'twere in scorn of eyes, reflecting gems,
That wooed the slimy bottom of the deep,
And mocked the dead bones that lay scattered by.

broken from the Tower escaped from my imprisonment in the Tower of London

Gloucester (who later became King Richard III)

hatches deck coverings

cited up recalled

heavy sad

wars of York and Lancaster Wars of the Roses

billows of the main waves of the sea

wracks wrecks

Inestimable innumerable

1 Use with Activity 2 on page 116 to help you prepare a choral-speaking presentation, with actions, echoes, repetitions, sound effects, etc.

2 Turn Clarence's story of his dream into an illustrated booklet. Each page of your booklet will contain one or more lines from the script together with your illustration of those lines.

The wounded Captain's story

USE WITH PAGE 116

In *Macbeth*, the wounded Captain tells King Duncan the story of the battle.

CAPTAIN Doubtful it stood,
As two spent swimmers that do cling together
And choke their art. The merciless Macdonald –
Worthy to be a rebel, for to that
The multiplying villainies of nature
Do swarm upon him – from the Western Isles
Of kerns and galloglasses is supplied,
And Fortune on his damnèd quarrel smiling,
Showed like a rebel's whore. But all's too weak,
For brave Macbeth – well he deserves that name –
Disdaining Fortune, with his brandished steel
Which smoked with bloody execution,
Like Valour's minion carved out his passage
Till he faced the slave,
Which ne'er shook hands, nor bade farewell to him,
Till he unseamed him from the nave to th'chaps
And fixed his head upon our battlements.

… Mark, King of Scotland, mark,
No sooner justice had, with valour armed,
Compelled these skipping kerns to trust their heels,
But the Norwegian lord, surveying vantage,
With furbished arms and new supplies of men
Began a fresh assault.

DUNCAN Dismayed not this our captains, Macbeth and Banquo?

CAPTAIN Yes, as sparrows, eagles, or the hare, the lion.
If I say sooth, I must report they were
As cannons over-charged with double cracks;
So they doubly redoubled strokes upon the foe.
Except they meant to bathe in reeking wounds
Or memorise another Golgotha,
I cannot tell.
But I am faint, my gashes cry for help.

Powerful simile! Two exhausted armies …

'swarm' is an image of bees – all over his body!

Should you point as you say this?

Nobody today knows what these are – how can you make the general sense clear to the audience?

Another vivid image! Fortune is like a prostitute who will favour anyone – however wicked.

kerns and galloglasses
lightly and heavily armed soldiers

Fortune
fickle luck

Valour's minion
bravery's favourite

nave to th'chaps
navel to the jaws

trust their heels
run away

surveying vantage
seeing an opportunity

furbished
polished, cleaned

sooth
truth

memorise another Golgotha
re-enact a slaughter like Christ's crucifixion

The lines have been partly marked up by a theatre director to help the actor with the language.

Use with Activity 2 on page 116 to help you mark up the rest of the wounded Captain's story in a similar way. Then act out the story.

Story: all in the Prologue !

USE WITH PAGE 116

In the Prologue to *Romeo and Juliet,* Chorus outlines the story of the play: how the bitter quarrels of the Montagues and Capulets were ended only by the death of their children, Romeo and Juliet.

Chorus
a narrator

misadventured
unlucky

overthrows
accidents

Two households, both alike in dignity,
In fair Verona (where we lay our scene),
From ancient grudge break to new mutiny,
Where civil blood makes civil hands unclean.
From forth the fatal loins of these two foes
A pair of star-crossed lovers take their life;
Whose misadventured piteous overthrows
Doth with their death bury their parents' strife.
The fearful passage of their death-marked love,
And the continuance of their parents' rage,
Which but their children's end nought could remove,
Is now the two hours' traffic of our stage;
The which if you with patient ears attend;
What here shall miss, our toil shall strive to mend.

1. Work in groups and use Activity 2 on page 116 to help you prepare your own short play to show all the actions described. One person as Chorus speaks a line at a time. After each line, the others act out what is described. For example, the mime for the first line could be a very stately, dignified parade of the two families, the Montagues and Capulets. For the second line you might show all kinds of activity in the main square of Verona: stall holders, customers, jugglers and other entertainers, tourists, etc.
2. In Baz Luhrmann's film of *Romeo and Juliet,* a television announcer spoke the Prologue as a TV news broadcast. How would you present the lines if you were making your own film of the play?

Opening scenes

USE WITH ONE OF PAGES 124 TO 126

As a playwright, Shakespeare knew that he must seize the interest and imagination of the audience right at the start of the play. Conflict must be introduced quickly, because it keeps the audience on the edge of their seats, eager to know what happens next. Who will win the battles of war and love, jealousy or justice?

At the start of each history play, ambitious nobles scheme and quarrel, or there is news of foreign wars. In the comedies, it is soon obvious that the course of true love will not run smooth. Each tragedy opens with a scene that sows the seeds of the catastrophes that will follow: Iago plots against Othello; Antony rejects Rome for Cleopatra; Hamlet's father's Ghost appears as Denmark prepares for war; King Lear rejects Cordelia and banishes Kent; the witches plan to meet Macbeth.

The opening of any play is an invitation to your imagination to work out how it might be staged. For example, *Hamlet* has been filmed many times. The opening sequences of different films have shown:

- battle scenes between Denmark and Norway, and Hamlet's father wounded
- Hamlet's funeral procession
- flags unfurling on the walls of Elsinore castle to signify old King Hamlet's death
- a chef peeping around a curtain to see if the next course can be served at an Elsinore banquet (to signify the theme of spying)
- Queen Gertrude weeping over the tomb of King Hamlet.

---

1. The language of the opening scene of every Shakespeare play creates an atmosphere, establishes a major theme, and predicts what the play will be about. Every new production aims to make the opening moments as gripping and dramatic as possible.

   Either, stage version: Take the opening scene of the play you are currently studying (or the one on the accompanying worksheet) and work out how you would perform it on stage.

   Or, film version: Plan the opening sequence of a film of a Shakespeare play. Your sequence accompanies the credits and leads up to the first line of the play.

2. How would you begin a play? Write the first twenty lines of a 'lost' Shakespeare play that you have just discovered.

Opening scenes: Macbeth

USE WITH PAGE 123

Three witches vow to meet Macbeth after the battle. Their familiar spirits call to them. As they leave, they chant ominous words.

Graymalkin/Paddock grey cat/toad (familiar spirits: demons who helped witches with their evil work)

Thunder and lightning. Enter three WITCHES

FIRST WITCH When shall we three meet again?
In thunder, lightning, or in rain?
SECOND WITCH When the hurly-burly's done,
When the battle's lost, and won.
THIRD WITCH That will be ere the set of sun.
FIRST WITCH Where the place?
SECOND WITCH Upon the heath.
THIRD WITCH There to meet with Macbeth.
FIRST WITCH I come, Graymalkin.
SECOND WITCH Paddock calls.
THIRD WITCH Anon.
ALL Fair is foul, and foul is fair,
Hover through the fog and filthy air.

Use with Activity 1 on page 123. Work in threes, or in larger groups. Learn the lines and act out the scene. Present it as dramatically as you can, together with sound effects: thunder, rain, battle sounds, cats, toads, etc.

Use your imagination on some of the following to create what you feel is the mood of the opening scene:

- How do the witches enter?
- How do they move?
- Are they old? young? male? female? (In Shakespeare's times they were played by males: in one modern production they were spiderwomen on a giant cobweb overhanging the stage.)
- Do they like or hate each other?
- How is each witch different from the others?
- How are they dressed? What are they carrying?
- Might they be father, mother and child?
- What do they do as they speak?

Opening scenes: Hamlet

USE WITH PAGE 123

It is midnight on a gun platform on the battlements of Elsinore castle. Francisco is on sentry duty. Barnardo comes to relieve him.

unfold
identify

rivals
partners

BARNARDO Who's there?
FRANCISCO Nay answer me. Stand and unfold yourself.
BARNARDO Long live the king!
FRANCISCO Barnardo?
BARNARDO He.
FRANCISCO You come most carefully upon your hour.
BARNARDO 'Tis now struck twelve, get thee to bed Francisco.
FRANCISCO For this relief much thanks, 'tis bitter cold
And I am sick at heart.
BARNARDO Have you had quiet guard?
FRANCISCO Not a mouse stirring.
BARNARDO Well, good night.
If you do meet Horatio and Marcellus,
The rivals of my watch, bid them make haste.
FRANCISCO I think I hear them.

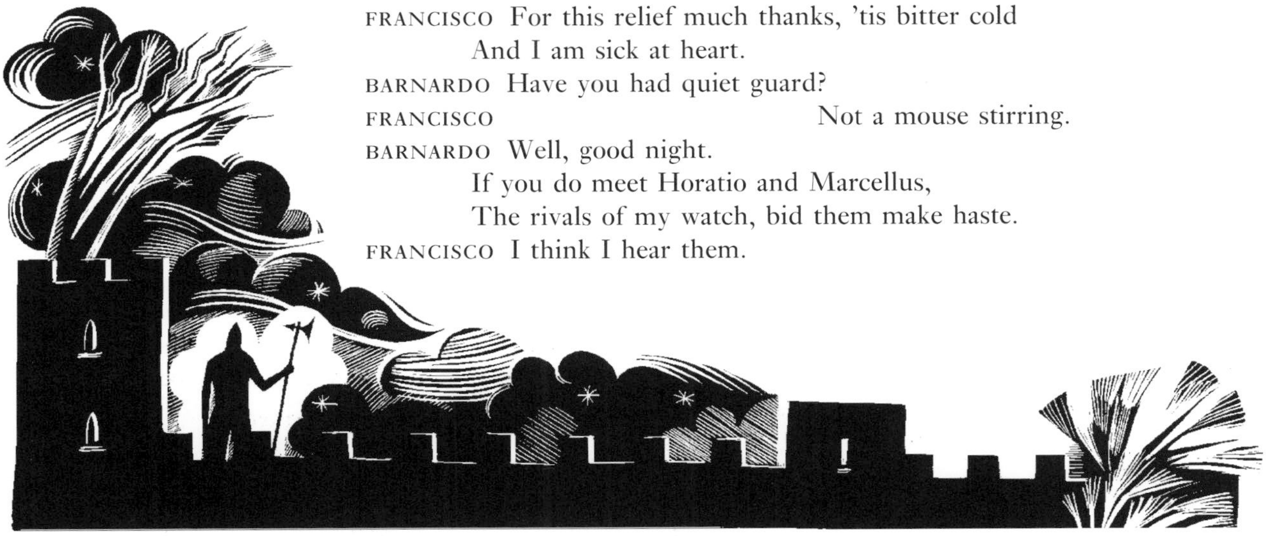

Use with Activity 1 on page 123. Explore possible answers to the following questions to help you heighten the dramatic effect of these opening lines:

- What will be the first thing the audience sees?
- How long a pause will there be before Barnardo speaks his first words?
- Why does Barnardo, the newcomer, challenge Francisco, contrary to military practice? (Francisco should challenge *him*.)
- How would you convince the audience that the night is bitterly cold?
- What sound effects would you use? What lighting effects?
- What accent or speech-style does each character use?
- It is just after midnight, dark but star-lit. How will you ensure the audience sees clearly what you want them to see?
- In Shakespeare's time, the play was staged in broad daylight. Identify all the words or phrases that help create the impression of night and darkness.
- What do the very short sentences suggest about the atmosphere?

Opening scenes: The Tempest

USE WITH PAGE 123

The Captain (Master) commands the Boatswain to save the ship from running aground. The Boatswain orders the courtiers back to their cabins.

A tempestuous noise of thunder and lightning.
Enter a SHIPMASTER, *a* BOATSWAIN *and* MARINERS

MASTER Boatswain!

BOATSWAIN Here, master. What cheer?

MASTER Good; speak to th'mariners. Fall to't yarely, or we run ourselves aground. Bestir, bestir!

Exit

BOATSWAIN Heigh, my hearts! Cheerly, cheerly, my hearts! Yare, yare! Take in the topsail. Tend to th'master's whistle [*To the storm*] Blow till thou burst thy wind, if room enough!

Enter ALONSO, SEBASTIAN, ANTONIO, FERDINAND, GONZALO *and others*

ALONSO Good boatswain, have care. Where's the master? Play the men.

BOATSWAIN I pray now, keep below.

ANTONIO Where is the master, boatswain?

BOATSWAIN Do you not hear him? You mar our labour – keep your cabins. You do assist the storm.

GONZALO Nay, good, be patient.

BOATSWAIN When the sea is. Hence! What cares these roarers for the name of king? To cabin. Silence! Trouble us not.

GONZALO Good, yet remember whom thou hast abroad.

BOATSWAIN None that I more love than myself. You are a councillor; if you can command these elements to silence, and work a peace of the present, we will not hand a rope more – use your authority. If you cannot, give thanks you have lived so long, and makè yourself ready in your cabin for the mischance of the hour, if it so hap. [*To the mariners*] Cheerly, good hearts. [*To the courtiers*] Out of our way, I say.

What cheer?
What news?

Good
Friend

Fall to't yarely
move smartly

Bestir
quickly

Tend
attend, listen

room
sea-room, space to sail in safety

Play the men
Act like men, command the sailors

keep below
stay in your cabins

mar
spoil, hinder

roarers
wild waves and winds

mischance
disaster

hap
happen

Work in large groups and use Activity 1 on page 123 to help you stage the scene to greatest dramatic effect. Try to show how the language helps create:

- the fury of the waves and wind
- the sense of fear and crisis
- the illusion of a ship caught in a tempest
- the challenge to traditional authority (the king and courtiers have to obey the Boatswain's orders).

Stage directions

USE WITH ONE OF PAGES 128 TO 131

The language of Shakespeare's playscripts is filled with stage directions for actors. When Macbeth says 'I drink to the general joy of the whole table', the action needed to accompany the line is clearly indicated in his words. In addition, every play contains explicit stage directions, for example:

- brief directions for actors:

  Enter, exit, exeunt (everyone leaves the stage)

  Alarms and excursions (the sounds and comings and goings of battle. In Shakespeare's time, it may have been the cue for an extended period of stage action depicting a battle scene).

- sound and other effects:

  Thunder and lightning. Enter three witches (Macbeth)

- other directions for dramatic effect:

  Exit, pursued by a bear (The Winter's Tale)

  Jupiter descends in thunder and lightning, sitting upon an eagle. He throws a thunderbolt. The ghosts fall on their knees. (Cymbeline)

  Thunder. Enter Third apparition, a child crowned, with a tree in his hand (Macbeth)

Every new production of The Winter's Tale *tries to find an exciting way of performing Shakespeare's most famous stage direction. It has been performed in many different ways, including:*

- *by an actor in a bear costume*
- *by a small actor dressed as a teddy bear, accompanied by the tune of* The Teddy Bear's Picnic
- *as an enormous shadow cast on the stage.*

1 Work out how you would stage each of the stage directions above, in a particular space in your school or college.

2 The single direction *Enter* is always an invitation to exercise your imagination. Just how does a king enter? How does a servant with only one line enter? The answer is different in every staging of each play. Sometimes characters do not speak for several minutes, but their actions establish what they are like. With this in mind, step into role and work on the following stage direction in *Hamlet*:

Enter two gravediggers

Stage directions: the Dumb Show

USE WITH PAGE 127

The Dumb Show, performed in *Hamlet*, is Shakespeare's longest stage direction.

Hoboys
oboes

makes show of protestation
shows her love

Anon
soon

mutes
silent actors

Hoboys play. The Dumb Show enters.

Enter a KING *and a* QUEEN, *very lovingly, the Queen embracing him. She kneels and makes show of protestation unto him. He takes her up, and declines his head upon her neck. He lies him down upon a bank of flowers. She, seeing him asleep, leaves him. Anon comes in another man, takes off his crown, kisses it, pours poison in the sleeper's ears, and leaves him. The Queen returns, finds the King dead, and makes passionate action. The poisoner, with some two or three mutes, comes in again, seeming to condole with her. The dead body is carried away. The poisoner woos the Queen with gifts. She seems harsh awhile, but in the end accepts his love.*

Exeunt

1. A Dumb Show is a mime of the action of the play that is to follow. To find how dramatically effective it can be – perform it!
2. Write and perform a Dumb Show of a scene from a popular television soap opera.

Stage directions: in the language

USE WITH PAGE 127

All stage directions have been removed from this extract from *Hamlet*, but the language itself contains many cues for action:

the rood
the holy cross of Christ

set those to you … speak
fetch the guards to correct you

ducat
gold coin ('I'll bet I've killed him')

POLONIUS He will come straight. Look you lay home to him.
Tell him his pranks have been too broad to bear with,
And that your grace hath screened and stood between
Much heat and him. I'll silence me e'en here.
Pray you be round with him.
HAMLET Mother, mother, mother!
GERTRUDE I'll warrant you, fear me not. Withdraw, I hear him coming.
HAMLET Now mother, what's the matter?
GERTRUDE Hamlet, thou hast thy father much offended.
HAMLET Mother, you have my father much offended.
GERTRUDE Come, come, you answer with an idle tongue.
HAMLET Go, go, you question with a wicked tongue.
GERTRUDE Why, how now Hamlet?
HAMLET What's the matter now?
GERTRUDE Have you forgot me?
HAMLET No by the rood, not so.
You are the queen, your husband's brother's wife,
And, would it were not so, you are my mother.
GERTRUDE Nay, then I'll set those to you that can speak.
HAMLET Come, come and sit you down, you shall not budge.
You go not till I set you up a glass
Where you may see the inmost part of you.
GERTRUDE What wilt thou do? thou wilt not murder me?
Help, help, ho!
POLONIUS What ho! Help, help, help!
HAMLET How now, a rat? Dead for a ducat, dead.
POLONIUS Oh, I am slain!
GERTRUDE Oh me, what hast thou done!
HAMLET Nay I know not, is it the king?
GERTRUDE Oh what a rash and bloody deed is this!
HAMLET A bloody deed? Almost as bad, good mother,
As kill a king and marry with his brother.
GERTRUDE As kill a king?
HAMLET Ay lady, 'twas my word.
Thou wretched, rash, intruding fool, farewell.
I took thee for thy better.

Shakespeare's language is filled with stage directions for actors. Write advice to the actors suggesting what they might do to accompany each line. Then take parts and act out the episode.

Stage directions: what Hamlet did

USE WITH PAGE 127

closet
private room

down-gyvèd
fallen (like fetters around his ankles)

purport
expression

perusal
study

bended their light
fixed his eyes

Ophelia tells how Hamlet visited her:

OPHELIA Oh my lord, my lord, I have been so affrighted.
POLONIUS With what, i'th'name of God?
OPHELIA My lord, as I was sewing in my closet,
Lord Hamlet with his doublet all unbraced,
No hat upon his head, his stockings fouled,
Ungartered, and down-gyvèd to his ankle,
Pale as his shirt, his knees knocking each other,
And with a look so piteous in purport
As if he had been loosèd out of hell
To speak of horrors – he comes before me.
POLONIUS Mad for thy love?
OPHELIA My lord I do not know,
But truly I do fear it.
POLONIUS What said he?
OPHELIA He took me by the wrist, and held me hard;
Then goes he to the length of all his arm,
And with his other hand thus o'er his brow
He falls to such perusal of my face
As he would draw it. Long stayed he so;
At last, a little shaking of mine arm,
And thrice his head thus waving up and down,
He raised a sigh so piteous and profound
As it did seem to shatter all his bulk,
And end his being. That done, he lets me go,
And with his head over his shoulder turned
He seemed to find his way without his eyes,
For out-a-doors he went without their helps
And to the last bended their light on me.

The Russian film of *Hamlet* actually shows on screen what Ophelia describes. Her lines are used as a voice-over to Hamlet's behaviour. How would you portray the episode?

Work in threes. As one person slowly speaks the lines, pausing after each short section, the other two, as Hamlet and Ophelia, mime the actions.

Stage directions: The Tempest

USE WITH PAGE 127

The Tempest contains more stage directions than any other play. Some people think that it is because Shakespeare wrote the play after he had retired to Stratford. Knowing he would not be present in rehearsal, he added more explicit stage directions than usual. Here are just a few from four episodes in the play:

- the shipwreck:

A tempestuous noise of thunder and lightning.
Enter a Shipmaster, a Boatswain and Mariners

Enter Mariners wet

- the Banquet:

Solemn and strange music, and Prospero, on the top, invisible

Enter several strange shapes, bringing in a banquet, and dance about it with gentle actions of salutations, and inviting the King, etc. to eat, they depart

Thunder and lightning. Enter ARIEL, *like a harpy, claps his wings upon the table, and with a quaint device the banquet vanishes*

Ariel vanishes in thunder; then, to soft music, enter the shapes again, and dance, with mocks and mows, and then depart carrying out the table.

harpy
monster in Greek mythology; part-woman, part-bird

mocks and mows
insulting gestures and faces

- the hunting of Caliban, Stephano and Trinculo:

A noise of hunters heard. Enter diverse spirits in shape of dogs and hounds, hunting them about. Prospero and Ariel setting them on

- the entry of the court:

Solemn music. PROSPERO *traces out a circle on stage. Here enters* ARIEL *before; then* ALONSO *with a frantic gesture, attended by* GONZALO, SEBASTIAN *and* ANTONIO *in like manner attended by* ADRIAN *and* FRANCISCO. *They all enter the circle which Prospero had made, and there stand charmed; which Prospero, observing, speaks*

Work out how you would stage four of these stage directions in a production of *The Tempest* in your own school or college.

Songs 1

USE WITH PAGE 133 OR 134

Twenty six of Shakespeare's thirty seven plays contain songs or fragments of songs. Each song contributes to the dramatic effect of the play in which it occurs, echoing a theme or giving insight into character and mood.

In Kenneth Branagh's film of *Much Ado About Nothing* the song 'Sigh no more, ladies' was shifted from its original position in Act 2 to the very opening of the film. It echoes the theme of love and untrustworthiness of Don John and Claudio, who, in very different ways, cause much unhappiness.

blithe and bonny
cheerful and carefree

no mo
no more

dumps
sad songs

fraud
faithlessness

Sigh no more, ladies, sigh no more,
Men were deceivers ever,
One foot in sea, and one on shore,
To one thing constant never.
Then sigh not so, but let them go,
And be you blithe and bonny,
Converting all your sounds of woe,
Into hey nonny nonny.

Sing no more ditties, sing no mo,
Of dumps so dull and heavy,
The fraud of men was ever so,
Since summer first was leavy,
Then sigh not so, but let them go,
And be you blithe and bonny,
Converting all your sounds of woe,
Into hey nonny nonny.

In Hamlet, the songs that Ophelia sings in her madness and grief reflect the events of the play and her own distracted state.

1 Make up your own music and perform the song. Don't be afraid to experiment with repeating lines or singing them in a different order.

2 For its 1993 production of *The Two Gentlemen of Verona*, the Royal Shakespeare Company added a further twelve love songs, for example, Cole Porter's *Night and day, In the still of the night, Love is the sweetest thing*. Baz Luhrmann's 1996 film of *Romeo and Juliet* used modern pop songs to intensify the mood of particular scenes.

Think of a few songs you could add to another Shakespeare play. Give reasons for your selection, and suggest the point in the play at which they would be sung, and the character who would sing them. You might wish to write your own song!

Songs 2

USE WITH PAGE 132

In *The Tempest* Ariel sings this song to Ferdinand. Its theme is how death magically transforms Ferdinand's father Alonso 'into something rich and strange'. The song forecasts what will happen in the play: Alonso, through suffering, will change for the better and regret his past wrongdoings.

knell
funeral bell

burden
refrain

Full fathom five thy father lies,
Of his bones are coral made;
Those are pearls that were his eyes;
Nothing of him that doth fade,
But doth suffer a sea-change
Into something rich and strange.
Sea-nymphs hourly ring his knell.
Hark, now I hear them, 'ding dong bell'.

[Spirits echo the burden 'ding dong bell']

In *A Midsummer Night's Dream* the fairies sing this song to their queen, Titania, to lull her to sleep.

Philomel
nightingale

FIRST FAIRY You spotted snakes with double tongue,
Thorny hedgehogs, be not seen.
Newts and blindworms, do no wrong,
Come not near our Fairy Queen.
CHORUS Philomel with melody
Sing in our sweet lullaby,
Lulla, lulla, lullaby; lulla, lulla, lullaby.
Never harm
Nor spell nor charm
Come our lovely lady nigh.
So good night, with lullaby.

FIRST FAIRY Weaving spiders, come not here;
Hence, you longlegged spinners, hence!
Beetles black approach not near;
Worm nor snail, do no offence.
CHORUS Philomel with melody
Sing in our sweet lullaby,
Lulla, lulla, lullaby; lulla, lulla, lullaby.
Never harm
Nor spell nor charm
Come our lovely lady nigh.
So good night, with lullaby.

Make up your own music and perform the songs. Don't be afraid to experiment with repeating lines or singing them in a different order.

Songs 3

USE WITH PAGE 132

In *As You Like It*, two Pages sing a song that echoes the themes of love and time.

ring time
the time for lovers to exchange rings

carol
ring dance

the prime
perfection, Spring

It was a lover and his lass,
With a hey, and a ho, and a hey nonino,
That o'er the green corn field did pass,
In the spring time, the only pretty ring time,
When birds do sing, hey ding a ding, ding,
Sweet lovers love the spring.

Between the acres of the rye,
With a hey, and a ho, and a hey nonino,
These pretty country folks would lie,
In spring time, the only pretty ring time,
When birds do sing, hey ding a ding, ding,
Sweet lovers love the spring.

This carol they began that hour,
With a hey, and a ho, and a hey nonino,
How that a life was but a flower,
In spring time, the only pretty ring time,
When birds do sing, hey ding a ding, ding,
Sweet lovers love the spring.

And therefore take the present time,
With a hey, and a ho, and a hey nonino,
For love is crownèd with the prime,
In spring time, the only pretty ring time,
When birds do sing, hey ding a ding, ding,
Sweet lovers love the spring.

Make up your own music and perform the song. A number of Shakespeare's songs are sung to traditional music, but don't be afraid to make up your own, and to repeat lines or sing them in a different order.

Insults 1

Shakespeare's plays are rich in insults. In *King Lear,* Kent insults Oswald:

worsted
woollen

action-taking
always going to law

glass-gazing
conceited, self admiring

superservicable
willing to serve in any way

finical
fussy

bawd/pander
pimp

addition
description

KENT Fellow, I know thee.
OSWALD What dost thou know me for?
KENT A knave, a rascal, an eater of broken meats, a base, proud, shallow, beggarly, three-suited, hundred-pound, filthy worsted-stocking knave; a lily-livered, action-taking, whoreson glass-gazing, superserviceable, finical rogue; one-trunk-inheriting slave; one that wouldst be a bawd in way of good service, and art nothing but the composition of a knave, beggar, coward, pander, and the son and heir of a mongrel bitch, one whom I will beat into clamorous whining if thou deniest the least syllable of thy addition.

1 Work with a partner. Use the lines from *King Lear* above and take turns at insulting each other! Accompany your words with appropriate gestures.

2 Divide the class into two groups on opposite sides of the room. Using the lines from *King Lear* above, each group speaks only up to a punctuation mark, then the other group speaks.

3 Invent your own list of insults, taking Kent's lines as your model.

Insults 2

Here are just a few things that Prince Hal and Falstaff call each other in *King Henry IV part 1*:

PRINCE Thou clay-brained guts

FALSTAFF You starveling

PRINCE Thou knotty-pated fool

FALSTAFF You elf-skin

PRINCE Thou whoreson obscene greasy tallow-catch

FALSTAFF You dried neat's-tongue

PRINCE Sanguine coward, bed-presser

FALSTAFF You bull's-pizzle

PRINCE Horse-back-breaker, huge hill of flesh

FALSTAFF You stock-fish!

PRINCE Bolting-hutch of beastliness, swollen parcel of dropsies

FALSTAFF O for a breath to utter what is like thee!

PRINCE Huge bombard of sack

FALSTAFF You tailor's-yard

PRINCE Stuffed cloak-bag of guts

FALSTAFF You sheath, you bow-case

PRINCE Roasted Manningtree ox with the pudding in his belly

FALSTAFF You vile standing tuck

PRINCE Reverend Vice, grey Iniquity, Father Ruffian, Vanity in years!

FALSTAFF You Prince of Wales!

PRINCE Why, you whoreson round man, what's the matter?

1. Work with a partner. Take parts and insult each other! Speak your words in a variety of ways: as a whisper, lovingly, sleepily and so on.
2. Divide the class into two groups on opposite sides of the room. One group is the Prince, the other is Falstaff. Exchange insults with accompanying gestures.

Insults: make up your own!

Column 1	Column 2	Column 3
simpering	languageless	block
painted	wasp-stung	drone
notable	lack-brained	lubber
threadbare	mad-headed	patch
decayed	shotten-herring	fancy-monger
flattering	nimble-footed	shoulder-clapper
shallow	puppy-headed	fragment
capering	fell-lurking	varlet
embossed	marble-hearted	popinjay
revolted	glass-gazing	mad wag
superfluous	outward-sainted	promise-breaker
meddling	lascivious	pander
counterfeit	strangely visited	coxcomb
twangling	lily-livered	hilding
juggling	cream-faced	mountebank
viperous	super-servicable	puke-stocking
venomous	frosty-spirited	basilisk
wretched	egregious	ticklebrain
slovenly	smooth-faced	bubble
manifest	whoreson	whey-face
scurvy	all-changing	horse-drench
odiferous	cony-catching	shrimp
abominable	hard-hearted	boggler
upstart	long-tongued	time-pleaser
malicious	pigeon-livered	Flibbertigibbet
juggling	skimble-skamble	whoremonger
unpolished	fustillarian	varlet
insinuating	hare-brained	bug
paltry	logger-headed	candle-maker
execrable	iron-witted	double-dealer
testy	foul-spoken	pantaloon
giddy	stretch-mouthed	boil

Choose one word from column 1, one from column 2 and one from column 3. Stroll around the room exchanging insults, or with a partner make up a conversation of insults. Every word is Shakespeare's!

Turning reading into drama

USE WITH ONE OF PAGES 139 TO 141

One of the great mysteries about William Shakespeare is that when he died, his will made no mention of the very valuable books he owned. Yet he was an avid reader, and every play shows evidence of the books he read.

Like every playwright, Shakespeare was constantly searching for new plots and fascinating characters. As a schoolboy his imagination was fired by the classical authors of Greece and Rome, particularly the Latin poet, Ovid. He used that school learning in his plays, transforming it into exciting drama.

Everything Shakespeare read fed his dramatic imagination: history books, other plays, pamphlets about current events, all kinds of stories, the romances of earlier times.

He found inspiration for his Roman plays (*Titus Andronicus, Julius Caesar, Antony and Cleopatra, Coriolanus*) in Plutarch's *Lives of the Greeks and Romans* which had been translated into English by Sir Thomas North in 1579.

For his plays about English history, Shakespeare ransacked Elizabethan history books. His particular favourite was Ralph Holinshed's C*hronicles of England, Scotland and Ireland*, published in 1587.

But Shakespeare was a playwright, not an historian. He was always concerned to use language and action on stage that would entertain and fascinate an audience. He did not give accurate historical accounts, but wrote plays that would seize the audience's imagination. He invented characters and scenes, rearranged the historical time of events to make them more dramatic, and left out or altered particular events and characters.

A brief phrase or sentence could trigger Shakespeare's dramatic creativity. For example, his inspiration for Lady Macbeth seems to have been a single sentence in Holinshed's *Chronicle*:

> The words of the three sisters greatly encouraged him hereunto, but specially his wife lay sore upon him to attempt the thing, she that was very ambitious, burning in unquenchable desire to bear the name of queen.

Shakespeare freely adapted what he read, but on the accompanying worksheet you can see how particular passages seized his imagination so strongly that he followed them closely as he turned them into poetic drama.

After you have worked on one of the worksheets, get together with a partner. One person steps into role as William Shakespeare. The other person takes the role of a critic who wishes to charge Shakespeare with plagiarism (copying someone else's writing and passing it off as your own).

Rewriting Cleopatra's barge

USE WITH PAGE 138

This is what Shakespeare read in Plutarch's *Lives*. It describes Cleopatra setting out to meet Mark Antony:

howboys
oboes

citherns
metal-stringed instruments like lutes or guitars

> She disdained to set forward otherwise but to take her barge in the river of Cydnus, the poop whereof was of gold, the sails of purple, and the oars of silver, which kept stroke in rowing after the sound of the music of flutes, howboys, citherns, viols, and such other instruments as they played upon in the barge. And now for the person of herself: she was laid under a pavilion of cloth of gold of tissue, apparelled and attired like the goddess Venus commonly drawn in picture; and hard by her, on either hand of her, pretty fair boys apparelled as painters do set forth god Cupid, with little fans in their hands, with the which they fanned wind upon her.

Here's how Shakespeare turned Plutarch's prose into verse:

burnished
polished, shining

poop
deck at stern

beggared all description
exhausts the power of language

cloth of gold, of tissue
very fine fabric

fancy outwork
imagination surpass

Cupids
gods of love

divers-coloured
iridescent, many changing colours

The barge she sat in, like a burnished throne
Burned on the water. The poop was beaten gold;
Purple the sails, and so perfumèd that
The winds were lovesick with them. The oars were silver,
Which to the tune of flutes kept stroke, and made
The water which they beat to follow faster,
As amorous of their strokes. For her own person,
It beggared all description: she did lie
In her pavilion – cloth of gold, of tissue –
O'erpicturing that Venus where we see
The fancy outwork nature. On each side her
Stood pretty dimpled boys, like smiling Cupids,
With divers-coloured fans, whose wind did seem
To glow the delicate cheeks which they did cool,
And what they undid did.

---

1 Speak both extracts aloud, then prepare an individual or choral presentation of Shakespeare's description.

2 Make a comparison of the two passages. Identify Shakespeare's additions, deletions, the changes he made to word order and so on. Add your own comments, giving your views on the poetic and dramatic quality of Shakespeare's changes.

Rewriting an ideal society

USE WITH PAGE 138

Part of an essay 'On Cannibals' by the French philosopher Michel de Montaigne influenced Shakespeare as he wrote *The Tempest*. Montaigne's essay was inspired by reports from explorers in the Americas who told of people ('noble savages') who lived in ideal natural societies, unspoilt by European civilisation.

intelligence knowledge

dividences social classes

> It is a nation … that hath no kind of traffic, no knowledge of letters, no intelligence of numbers, no name of magistrate nor of politic superiority, no use of service, of riches or poverty, no contracts, no successions, no dividences, no occupation but idle, no respect of Kindred but common, no apparel but natural, no manuring of lands, no use of wine, corn or metal. The very words that import lying, falsehood, treasons, envy, dissimulation; covetousness, detraction, and pardon were never heard.

Shakespeare used Montaigne's essay as he wrote Gonzalo's picture of a society in which ownership of everything is shared ('commonwealth').

contraries opposite to the usual custom

Execute organise

traffic commerce, trade

Letters education

use of service slavery, servants

contract, succession inheritance

Bourn, bound of land, tilth boundaries, fences, agriculture

sovereignty kings

engine weapon

foison plenty

I'th'commonwealth I would by contraries
Execute all things. For no kind of traffic
Would I admit; no name of magistrate;
Letters should not be known; riches, poverty,
And use of service, none; contract, succession,
Bourn, bound of land, tilth, vineyard, none;
No use of metal, corn, or wine, or oil;
No occupation, all men idle, all;
And women too, but innocent and pure;
No sovereignty –

All things in common nature should produce
Without sweat or endeavour. Treason, felony,
Sword, pike, knife, gun, or need of any engine
Would I not have; but nature should bring forth
Of it own kind, all foison, all abundance
To feed my innocent people.

1 Speak both extracts aloud, then make a comparison by copying and completing the table below:

Montaigne	Shakespeare	Comment
Nation	commonwealth	Shakespeare chooses a more precise word
	I would by contraries … things	Shakespeare adds a generalisation
no kind of traffic	no kind of traffic	

2 Use your completed table to write several paragraphs giving your own response to Shakespeare's changes.

Rewriting history into drama

USE WITH PAGE 138

A passage from Holinshed's *Chronicles* describes how Macbeth and Banquo met the three witches:

elder
supernatural

> It fortuned as Macbeth and Banquo journied towards Forres, where the King then lay, they went sporting by the way together without other company save only themselves, passing through the woods and fields, when suddenly in the midst of a land, there met them three women in strange and wild apparel, resembling creatures of elder world, whom when they attentively beheld, wondering much at the sight, the first of them spake and said: All hail Macbeth, thane of Glamis (for he had lately entered into that dignity and office by the death of his father Sinel). The second of them said: Hail Macbeth, thane of Cawdor. But the third said: All hail Macbeth that hereafter shall be King of Scotland.

Here's how Shakespeare turned the passage into gripping drama:

aught
anything

Glamis
(pronounced Glahms, one syllable)

MACBETH So foul and fair a day I have not seen.
BANQUO How far is't called to Forres? What are these,
So withered and so wild in their attire,
That look not like th'inhabitants o'th'earth,
And yet are on't? – Live you, or are you aught
That man may question? You seem to understand me,
By each at once her choppy finger laying
Upon her skinny lips; you should be women
And yet your beards forbid me to interpret
That you are so.
MACBETH Speak if you can: what are you?
FIRST WITCH All hail Macbeth, hail to thee, Thane of Glamis.
SECOND WITCH All hail Macbeth, hail to thee, Thane of Cawdor.
THIRD WITCH All hail Macbeth, that shalt be king hereafter.

Read both versions aloud, then step into role as William Shakespeare. Explain, line by line, what went through your mind as you rewrote Holinshed. Remember, as a playwright, you are always asking yourself: 'How can I put this on stage to greatest dramatic effect?'

Revising: Quarto and Folio

USE WITH PAGE 143

Did Shakespeare revise his plays? No-one knows for certain, but it seems likely that he did. For example, two versions of *King Lear* exist: a Quarto version published in 1608, and the Folio version of 1623. (The words quarto and folio refer to the size of the page: quarto is approximately half the size of this sheet; folio is about twice the size of this sheet.)

The Folio cuts out 300 lines included in the Quarto, but adds 100 new lines. No-one can be sure why Shakespeare altered his play, or which of the versions he preferred. Perhaps he was anxious not to offend the authorities in case they decided to impose censorship. For example, the Folio version cuts the lines in which King Lear is called a fool.

Shakespeare may have felt that he could increase dramatic effect by his changes. Perhaps he shortened the play to prepare a touring version for performances outside London.

The Quarto may be an illegal publication based on a stolen copy of Shakespeare's working script. The Folio may be Shakespeare's final thoughts on the play, but it is quite possible that someone else, not Shakespeare, prepared the Folio version for publication. Shakespeare died in 1616, seven years before the Folio was published.

1 Use the extracts from the Folio and Quarto on the accompanying worksheet.

King Lear has divided his kingdom into three parts. He asks each of his three daughters to declare how much they love him. The daughter who expresses most love will receive the greatest share of land. The two elder daughters, Gonerill and Regan, speak first and Lear rewards them. The extracts begin when he then speaks to Cordelia.

Take parts as Lear and Cordelia and speak each version.

2 Copy and complete the table below, listing the differences between the Quarto and the Folio versions. Suggest why you think each change was made. If you were preparing the play for performance, what would *your* audience hear? Make your choices – then rehearse and stage your version.

Quarto (1608)	Folio (1623)	Possible reason for change	My recommendation for performance

Quarto version 1608 (spelling modernised)

USE WITH PAGE 142

LEAR but now our joy,
Although the last, not least in our dear love,
What can you say to win a third, more opulent
Than your sisters.

CORDELIA Nothing my lord.

LEAR How, nothing can come of nothing, speak again.

CORDELIA Unhappy that I am, I cannot heave my heart into my mouth, I love your majesty according to my bond, no more nor less.

LEAR Go to, go to, mend your speech a little,
Lest it may mar your fortunes.

CORDELIA Good my lord,
You have begot me, bred me, loved me,
I return those duties back as are right fit,
Obey you, love you, and most honour you,
Why have my sisters husbands if they say they love you all,
Happily when I shall wed, that lord whose hand
Must take my plight, shall carry half my love with him,
Half my care and duty, sure I shall never
Marry like my sisters, to love my father all.

LEAR But goes this with thy heart?

CORDELIA Ay good my lord.

LEAR So young and so untender.

CORDELIA So young my lord and true.

Folio version 1623 (spelling modernised)

LEAR Now our joy,
Although our last and least, to whose young love,
The vines of France, and milk of Burgundy,
Strive to be interessed. What can you say, to draw
A third more opulent than your sisters? Speak.

CORDELIA Nothing my lord.

LEAR Nothing?

CORDELIA Nothing.

LEAR Nothing will come of nothing, speak again.

CORDELIA Unhappy that I am, I cannot heave
My heart into my mouth: I love your majesty
According to my bond, no more nor less.

LEAR How, how, Cordelia? Mend your speech a little,
Lest you may mar your fortunes.

CORDELIA Good my lord,
You have begot me, bred me, loved me.
I return those duties back as are right fit,
Obey you, love you, and most honour you.
Why have my sisters husbands, if they say
They love you all? Happily, when I shall wed,
That lord, whose hand must take my plight, shall carry
Half my love with him, half my care, and duty,
Sure I shall never marry like my sisters.

LEAR But goes thy heart with this?

CORDELIA Ay my good lord.

LEAR So young, and so untender?

CORDELIA So young my lord, and true.

interessed
admitted, married (the king of France and the Duke of Burgundy are suitors to Cordelia)

opulent
rich

bond
duties as a daughter

mar
damage

begot
fathered

Shakespeare's language: some technical terms

More information and examples can be found on the pages shown after each item.

alarms and excursions a stage direction meaning the sounds and actions of battle: trumpets, drums and skirmishes on stage (page 127)

alliteration the repetition of consonants, usually at the beginning of words (pages 14, 21)

antithesis the opposition of words or phrases against each other in balanced contrast (pages 12–13)

apostrophe addressing an object or person as if they were actually present ('O Wall!')

aside a brief remark by a character, usually to the audience, unheard by other characters

assonance the repetition of vowel sounds (pages 14, 21)

blank verse unrhymed verse written in *iambic pentameter* (pages 28–35)

bombast boastful or ranting language (page 54)

caesura a pause in a line of verse (page 30)

chiasmus a mirror image type of *antithesis* where one phrase is the reverse of the other: 'Love's fire heats water, water cools not love' (pages 12–13)

Chorus a narrator who introduces or comments on the play: as in *Romeo and Juliet* and *Henry V*. In *Pericles*, Gower acts as Chorus. (pages 96, 122)

conceit a very elaborate image (see *imagery*)

deixis such words as I, he, she, them, it, there, then, etc. These words tell who or what is the person, thing, place or time referred to. (pages 62–63)

dialogue verbal exchange between two or more characters on stage (pages 68–76)

end-stopped lines a line of verse that makes sense on its own, with a clear pause at the end of the line (page 28)

enjambement verse in which the sense runs on from one line to the next; lines which are not *end-stopped* (page 28)

epilogue a speech to the audience at the end of the play, often asking for applause, as in *As You Like It, All's Well That Ends Well, A Midsummer Night's Dream, Henry V, Henry IV part 2*, Henry *VIII, Pericles, Twelfth Night* (a song), *The Tempest*

exeunt a stage direction meaning 'everyone leaves the stage'

feminine ending line of verse in *iambic pentameter* with an additional unstressed syllable at the end of the line ('To be, or not to be, that is the question')

folio a large sheet of paper, about twice the size of this sheet. The First Folio is the collection of all Shakespeare's plays published in 1623. (pages 142–143)

hyperbole extravagant and obviously exaggerated language: 'hype' (pages 52–53)

iamb a metrical unit of two syllables, the first unstressed, the second stressed: the regular rhythm of *blank verse* (listen to your heart-beat! di *dum*, di *dum*, di *dum* ...)

iambic pentameter a ten syllable line of verse with five stresses: di *dum*, di *dum*, di *dum*, di *dum*, di *dum* (pages 28–35)

imagery the use of emotionally charged words and phrases that conjure up vivid mental pictures in the imagination (pages 1–11)

irony saying one thing but meaning another: verbal irony; a strong contrast with what happens elsewhere in the play: dramatic irony (pages 56–58)

iterative imagery repeated *imagery*, images which recur throughout the play (pages 1–11)

line the basic unit of verse

malapropism inappropriate, muddled or mistaken use of words (page 60)

masculine ending a stressed syllable ending a verse line

metaphor a comparison that suggests two dissimilar things are actually the same (page 1)

metre how the rhythm of verse is measured; the inner rhythmical structure of a line (see *pentameter*, *tetrameter*) (pages 28–37)

onomatopoeia words whose sound mimic what they describe (page 21)

oxymoron two incongruous or contradictory words brought together to make a striking expression: 'cold fire'; 'sweet sorrow' (page 59)

parody a mocking imitation of a particular style of language use (page 15)

pentameter the rhythm of a verse line with five stresses (penta = five) (page 28)

personification turning all kinds of things – death, time, war, love, England, etc. – into persons, giving them human feelings and attributes (page 11)

prologue the introduction to a play, spoken by *Chorus* in *Henry V* and *Romeo and Juliet*, and by Rumour in *Henry IV part 2* (page 122)

prose all language not in verse. Used mainly, but not always, for comedy, madness, low status characters, letters and proclamations. (pages 40–45)

pun wordplay: when a word has two or more different meanings the ambiguity can be used for comic or serious effect (page 55)

quarto a sheet of paper about half the size of this sheet. Around half Shakespeare's plays were published during his lifetime in Quarto editions (pages 142–143)

rhetoric the art of persuasion (pages 46–51)

rhyme matching sounds at the end of verse lines (pages 38–39)

run-on lines see *enjambement*

shared lines where a line is shared between two or more speakers (page 33)

simile a comparison using 'like' or 'as' (page 1)

soliloquy a speech by a character who is alone, or believes himself or herself to be alone, on stage. Often a kind of internal debate (pages 77–84)

sonnet a poem of fourteen lines written in *iambic pentameter*

stichomythia rapidly alternating single lines spoken by two characters (pages 68, 70)

syntax the structure of sentences; the way in which words are arranged in a sentence

tetrameter the rhythm of a verse line with four stresses (pages 36–37)

verse strongly patterned language. The typical Shakespearean pattern is *blank verse*: each line has ten syllables and five stresses (see *iambic pentameter*). (pages 28–37)

Index of extracts

Extracts

There are obvious problems in extracting speeches or short episodes from Shakespeare's plays. When the play is performed on stage, speech and silence, action and reaction, scene and scene, are closely intertwined, and all are given greater significance by the experience of the whole performance. To detach a single speech or scene from its total dramatic context, clearly therefore has drawbacks. It is with an awareness of such limitations that this collection has been compiled.

But extracts do have advantages for the study of Shakespeare's language in school and college classrooms. They encourage imaginative inference and deduction; they allow students to explore in depth one or more particular features of language; and they offer fruitful opportunities for active group work.

Within the compass of a lesson, teachers can ensure that students are able to share the results of their work on a chosen extract. In that shared experience, students can more fully understand and appreciate the range of responses that Shakespeare's language so excitingly invites and encourages.

Where a worksheet contains more than one extract, however short, each is listed in the order in which it appears on the worksheet. Each extract is identified by Act, Scene and line number (for example, *King Lear* 4.6.42–45 is Act 4 Scene 6 lines 42–45). All references are to the *New Cambridge/Cambridge School Shakespeare* edition, with the exception of the following:

As You Like It; Coriolanus; Cymbeline; Henry VIII; Love's Labour's Lost; Richard III; Titus Andronicus; Timon of Athens; Troilus and Cressida

21 *Twelfth Night* 3.4.120; *King John* 5.2.117; *Macbeth* 1.3.33–34; *King Lear* 4.5.20–21; *A Midsummer Night's Dream* 5.1.145–146

22 *Macbeth* 4.3.57–60; *Richard III* 4.4.169–172; *The Merchant of Venice* 3.1.46–50; *Henry V* 4.8.84–89

23 *Macbeth* 4.1.1–21

24 *Much Ado About Nothing* 2.1.199–205; *Romeo and Juliet* 4.1.77–85

25 *The Comedy of Errors* 5.1.237–242; 1.2.97–102; *Richard II* 2.1.40–50

26 *Much Ado About Nothing* 5.1.190–197

27 *King John* 4.2.182–202

28 *Romeo and Juliet* 2.2.2; *Titus Andronicus* 5.3.185–188; *Macbeth* 5.3.22–23

29 *Hamlet* 4.7.166–183

30 *Othello* 5.2.1–22

31 *Richard II* 3.3.143–159

32 *A Midsummer Night's Dream* 1.1.180–203

33 *Antony and Cleopatra* 4.4.4–11; *King John* 3.3.66

34 *Romeo and Juliet* 2.2.2–6; *Romeo and Juliet* Prologue 1–14; *Twelfth Night* 1.1.1–15

35 *Romeo and Juliet* 4.3.30–48; 1.1.72–79; 1.1.80–94; 1.1.164–173

36 *Macbeth* 4.1.4–5; *Sonnet 145*

37 *A Midsummer Night's Dream* 5.1.349–368; 2.1.2–15

38 *Macbeth* 1.1.1–2; 2.1.63–64; *Love's Labour's Lost* 1.1.84–99

39 *Much Ado About Nothing* 5.2.28–31; *A Midsummer Night's Dream* 5.1.306–329

41 *The Comedy of Errors* 4.4.29–34; *Macbeth* 2.3.23–30

42 *Much Ado About Nothing* 2.3.7–27

43 *Hamlet* 3.2.1–36

44 *Hamlet* 2.2.280–291

45 *King Lear* 3.4.49–58; 115–116

46 *Macbeth* 2.3.99–111

47 *Henry V* 3.1.1–34

48 *Julius Caesar* 3.2.13–34

49 *Julius Caesar* 3.2.65–99

50 *Macbeth* 1.7.1–28

51 *Macbeth* 1.7.35–59

52 *Othello* 5.2.277–278; *Antony and Cleopatra* 5.2.81–91

53 *The Merchant of Venice* 3.2.114–129

54 *A Midsummer Night's Dream* 1.2.24–27; *Hamlet* 5.1.236–251

55 *Love's Labour's Lost* 5.2.686–687; *Henry V* 5.1.75–76; *Othello* 5.2.7; *Romeo and Juliet* 3.1.89–90; *The Taming of the Shrew* 1.2.1–19

56 *Macbeth* 1.6.1; *Twelfth Night* 3.1.126; *Othello* 1.1.66

57 *Romeo and Juliet* 3.5.78–102

58 *Julius Caesar* 1.2.233–265

59 *Romeo and Juliet* 2.2.184; 1.1.166–172; 3.2.73–79;

60 *Much Ado About Nothing* 3.3.1–22

61 *The Two Gentlemen of Verona* 4.2.85–97

62 *Sonnet 42*

63 *Romeo and Juliet* 5.3.231–264

65 *All's Well That Ends Well* 4.1.52–53

68 *Hamlet* 3.4.8–12; *As You Like It* 5.3.78–83

69 *Hamlet* 5.1.99–131

70 *Macbeth* 2.2.8–37

71 *King Lear* 2.4.223–256

72 *Much Ado About Nothing* 4.1.248–279

73 *A Midsummer Night's Dream* 1.1.128–149

74 *Henry V* 5.1.20–60

75 *Hamlet* 4.3.16–49

76 *The Comedy of Errors* 3.2.89–124

77 *Richard III* 1.1.30

78 *Richard III* 5.5.131–160

79 *Hamlet* 3.1.56–88

80 *The Two Gentlemen of Verona* 4.4.1–32

81 *Romeo and Juliet* 3.2.1–31

82 *Macbeth* 2.1.33–64

83 *The Tempest* 5.1.33–57

84 *Henry IV part 2* 3.1.4–31

85 *Romeo and Juliet* 1.1.58

86 *Romeo and Juliet* 1.3.17–49

87 *Hamlet* 1.2.129–159

88 *King Henry IV part 1* 1.3.199–205; 5.1.125–138

89 *The Tempest* 1.2.332–345; 3.2.130–138

90 *Othello* 3.4.51–64; 4.1.35–41

91 *Henry IV part 2* 2.1.65–80

92 *Richard III* 1.1.1–31

93 *Hamlet* 3.1.131–155

94 *Julius Caesar* 1.2.192–214

95 *Henry V* Prologue 26–27; *Hamlet* 3.3.349–351; *King Lear* 3.2.1–13; *Romeo and Juliet* 4.3.33–34

96 *Henry V* Prologue 1–31

97 *Cymbeline* 4.2.259–282; *Romeo and Juliet* 4.5.84–90

98 *Romeo and Juliet* 4.3.30–58

99 *Macbeth* 1.5.39–52; 3.2.46–53

100 *King Lear* 3.2.1–23

101 *Macbeth* 2.3.59–74

102 *King Lear* 4.5.11–24

103 *The Merchant of Venice* 5.1.54–65

104 *The Winter's Tale* 5.3.85–109

106 *The Merchant of Venice* 3.2.73–98

107 *King Lear* 4.5.144–164

108 *Twelfth Night* 2.2.14–38

109 *Troilus and Cressida* 1.3.94–110

110 *Henry VI part 3* 2.5.1–13

111 *Hamlet* 5.1.146–165

112 *The Two Gentlemen of Verona* 2.1.15–27

113 *Measure for Measure* 5.1.402–404

114 *Romeo and Juliet* 3.5.137–168

115 *As You Like It* 2.7.139–166

117 *The Tempest* 1.2.194–215

118 *Hamlet* 1.5.59–80

119 *Macbeth* 5.1.27–58

120 *Richard III* 1.4.9–33

121 *Macbeth* 1.2.7–42

122 *Romeo and Juliet* Prologue 1–14

124 *Macbeth* 1.1.1–13

125 *Hamlet* 1.1.1–14

126 *The Tempest* 1.1.1–24

127 *Macbeth* 3.4.89; 1.1.1; *The Winter's Tale* 3.3.57; *Cymbeline* 5.5.186; *Macbeth* 4.1.85

128 *Hamlet* 3.2.120

129 *Hamlet* 3.4.1–32

130 *Hamlet* 2.1.73–98

131 *The Tempest* 1.1.1; 1.1.45; 3.3.17; 3.3.19; 3.3.52; 3.3.82; 4.1.252; 5.1.57

132 *Much Ado About Nothing* 2.3.53–68

133 *The Tempest* 1.2.396–403; *A Midsummer Night's Dream* 2.2.9–30

134 *As You Like It* 5.3.15–38

135 *King Lear* 2.2.11–21

136 *King Henry IV part 1* throughout 2.4

139 *Antony and Cleopatra* 2.2.201–215

140 *The Tempest* 2.1.142–158

141 *Macbeth* 1.3.36–48

143 *King Lear* 1.1.77–101

Index of plays

William Shakespeare 1564-1616

1564 Born Stratford-upon-Avon, eldest son of John and Mary Shakespeare.

1582 Marries Anne Hathaway of Shottery, near Stratford.

1583 Daughter, Susanna, born.

1585 Twins, son and daughter, Hamnet and Judith, born.

1592 First mention of Shakespeare in London. Robert Greene, another playwright, described Shakespeare as 'an upstart crow beautified with our feathers ...'. Greene seems to have been jealous of Shakespeare. He mocked Shakespeare's name, calling him 'the only Shake-scene in the country' (presumably because of Shakespeare's successful plays).

1595 A shareholder in 'The Lord Chamberlain's Men', an acting company that became extremely popular.

1596 Son Hamnet dies, aged eleven.

Father, John, granted arms (acknowledged as a gentleman).

1597 Bought New Place, the grandest house in Stratford.

1598 Acted in Ben Jonson's *Every Man in His Humour.*

1599 Globe Theatre opens on Bankside. Performances in the open air.

1601 Father, John, dies.

1603 James I grants Shakespeare's company a royal patent: 'The Lord Chamberlain's Men' became 'The King's Men' and played about twelve performances each year at court.

1607 Daughter, Susanna, marries Dr John Hall.

1608 Mother, Mary, dies.

1609 'The King's Men' begin performing indoors at Blackfriars Theatre.

1610 Probably returned from London to live in Stratford.

1616 Daughter, Judith, marries Thomas Quiney.

Died. Buried in Holy Trinity Church, Stratford-upon-Avon.

The plays and poems (no one knows exactly when he wrote each play)

1589-1595 *The Two Gentlemen of Verona*, *The Taming of the Shrew*, *First, Second and Third Parts of King Henry VI*, *Titus Andronicus*, *King Richard III*, *The Comedy of Errors*, *Love's Labour's Lost*, *A Midsummer Night's Dream*, *Romeo and Juliet*, *King Richard II* (and the long poems *Venus and Adonis* and *The Rape of Lucrece*).

1596-1599 *King John*, *The Merchant of Venice*, *First and Second Parts of King Henry IV*, *The Merry Wives of Windsor*, *Much Ado About Nothing*, *King Henry V*, *Julius Caesar* (and probably the *Sonnets*).

1600-1605 *As You Like It*, *Hamlet*, *Twelfth Night*, *Troilus and Cressida*, *Measure for Measure*, *Othello*, *All's Well That Ends Well*, *Timon of Athens*, *King Lear.*

1606-1611 *Macbeth*, *Antony and Cleopatra*, *Pericles*, *Coriolanus*, *The Winter's Tale*, *Cymbeline*, *The Tempest.*

1613 *King Henry VIII*, *The Two Noble Kinsmen* (both probably with John Fletcher).

1623 Shakespeare's plays published as a collection (now called the First Folio).

Political and other events

1564 Michelangelo dies; Galileo and Christopher Marlowe born

1565 Potatoes and tobacco introduced into England

1572 St Bartholomew's Day massacre of French Protestants in Paris

1579 Sir Francis Drake claims English sovereignty over New Albion (California)

1580 Drake completes his voyage around the world

1586 Death of Sir Philip Sidney, famous courtier, poet, soldier and statesman

1587 Mary Queen of Scots executed; Marlowe's *Tamburlaine* begins a series of big stage successes

1588 Defeat of the Spanish Armada

1591 Sir Philip Sidney's sonnet sequence published, sparking off an intense period of sonnet writing; Christopher Marlowe killed in tavern brawl

1592 Philip Henslowe, London theatre manager, begins keeping his diary until 1603; plague kills 15000 people in London

1593 London theatres closed by plague

1594 Period of poor harvests begins; Dr Lopez executed for alleged attempt to assassinate Queen Elizabeth

1596 Sir Walter Raleigh's *Discovery of Guiana* published

1599 Globe Theatre opens on Bankside; Earl of Essex' expedition to Ireland fails; Oliver Cromwell born; King James VI of Scotland (later King James I of England) asserts Divine Right of Kings

1600 Will Kemp, once a famous clown in Shakespeare's plays, dances from London to Norwich

1601 Earl of Essex executed for leading a revolt against Queen Elizabeth

1603 Queen Elizabeth dies; King James succeeds to the throne

1605 Gunpowder Plot

1606 Companies formed to take English colonists to the New World (America)

1607 English establish first permanent American settlement at Jamestown

1609 Colonists bound for Virginia shipwrecked on Bermuda (their story became a source for *The Tempest*)

1611 King James dissolves Parliament; Authorised Version of the Bible published: 'King James Bible'

1612 Last recorded burning of heretics in England

1613 Globe Theatre burned down during performance of Henry VIII

1614 Globe Theatre rebuilt; American Indian Princess Pocahontas marries Englishman John Rolfe

1619 Actor Richard Burbage dies – he had created many of Shakespeare's most famous heroic roles

Portrait of Shakespeare by Martin Droeshout from the title-page of the First Folio, 1623